BOOKS AND BOOK-COLLECTING

BOOKS AND
BOOK-COLLECTING

G. L. BROOK

ANDRE DEUTSCH
A GRAFTON BOOK

First published 1980 by
André Deutsch Limited
105 Great Russell Street London WC1

Printed in Great Britain by
Willmer Brothers Limited Rock Ferry Merseyside

British Library Cataloguing in Publication Data
Brook, George Leslie
    Books and book-collecting. – (Grafton books
    on library and information science).
    1. Book-collecting
    I. Title
    020'.75   Z987

ISBN 0 233 97154 8

This book is set in 12/13pt. Monotype Bembo.

The device on the title page is that of Aldus Manutius
who printed the *De Aetna* by Pietro Bembo in 1495–6
from type he commissioned specially from Francesco Griffo.
Monotype Bembo is modelled on Griffo's original design.

TO
CHRISTOPHER BROOK WALKER

CONTENTS

CHAPTER I

HAVE YOU READ THEM ALL?

A NYONE who buys a large number of books has to be prepared to hear the question which gives its title to this chapter repeatedly posed by visitors. The following dialogue is typical of scores in which I have taken part:

> *Man delivering carpet:* 'I should just like to say that I have never seen such a smashing library.'
> No reply from me.
> 'And presumably you have read every one of them.'
> 'No.'
> I was conscious that I had let him down, and there was a marked drop in temperature as he said: 'Mmm, pity.'

The first thing that should be said about this question is that it is purely rhetorical. The man or woman who asks it doesn't really want to know whether you have read all your books; he is pretty certain that you have not. He could become quite certain if he devoted three minutes' thought to the subject but, in the words of A. E. Housman, thought is irksome and three minutes is a long time. Only a fool would try to read through the *Concise Oxford Dictionary* or *Whitaker's Almanack*, fascinating as both books are for browsing in. Very few people indeed have read all their books, except those who, like Thackeray's Major Ponto, have libraries that are 'small but well-selected' almost to the point of non-existence.

The words 'Have you read them all?' are not a question but a reproach, though one that does not necessarily involve hostility. What the speaker means is: 'I know your sort. You give yourself airs because you have a lot of books, but mere possession is nothing to be proud of if you have not read them.' Like Jaques in *As You Like It* he seeks reassurance by saying 'I think of as many matters as he; but I give heaven thanks, and make no boast of them'. The reproach contains more than a germ of truth; undoubtedly books are meant to be read, but the question 'Have you read them all?' is superficial because it concentrates on only one of the many reasons for possessing books. In fact, one of the many replies that I have given to this question is: 'Of course not. If I had read them, what would be the point of keeping them?' The fallacy of this reply is obvious, but its justification is that when you get a silly question you can give a silly answer.

You can, of course, enumerate several reasons for possessing books that you have never read. An obvious one is that you intend to read them at some unspecified time in the future. It is especially true of second-hand books but it is true to some extent of new ones that a buyer has to seize opportunities when they arise. He cannot count on being able to buy a particular book just when he wants to read it.

One category of unread books consists of works of reference like gazetteers or dictionaries, but there are many other books which could be read through but which most people who are not specialists would prefer to treat as works of reference.

Another reason for possessing an unread book is that we intend to pass it on to someone else. Our motives for buying books in this category vary from disinterested love of our fellow-men down to a desire to make a tax-free profit on resale and to deprive hard-working second-hand booksellers of their legitimate gains. Book-buyers vary a good deal in the extent to which they buy books for this reason. There are single-minded men and women who are content to ignore all books that they do not want to read or keep for reference, but there are others whose interests are wider. Anyone who frequents bookshops or reads about books acquires a good deal of miscellaneous knowledge about the rarity of particular books and the eccentricities of particular booksellers. The knowledge may be unnecessary to him because the book is outside his own field or because he already has a copy, but if he comes across a book that turns up only once every ten years at a price that he can afford, he should not be so self-centred as to refuse to buy it for a friend or so disinterested as to refuse to turn amateur bookseller and to back his judgement with a view to financial profit. In thus entering into competition with the booksellers he is not likely to endear himself to them, but he is not an unmitigated nuisance. The bookseller who ultimately relieves him of his purchase may be assumed to be buying the book because it pays him to do so. If it were not for the activities of the amateur bookseller, whom I prefer to regard as a bee, flying beneficently from flower to flower, it is unlikely that the bookseller would have the time to hunt out all the bargains for himself. It may be said that buying books for resale does not account for keeping them on one's shelves for a long time, but to the amateur bookseller, as to the professional, willingness to wait is essential to success. The successful practitioner learns to recognize a rising market. To mention only two categories, the history of science and manuscripts of contemporary authors are both fields in which prices have often advanced more than twenty-fold in the last forty years. There are other reasons for buying books that we do not intend to read. The real justification of the book-collector in society, the thing that allows him to feel a bit superior to the collector of tram-tickets or matchbox labels, is that he is forming a collection that may be of real value to the scholar of the future. In order to achieve this aim he does not necessarily have to buy a lot of books, but he must specialize in a field small enough to make some sort of completeness possible, or at least in his chosen field he must include a number of books that are not easily to be found even in a large library. This is a laudable aim which many people who possess thousands of books do not care to achieve, but a man may form a collection of the greatest value to scholars even if he never opens a single volume of his collection. This is true not only of the Folgers and the Huntingtons, but also of the man who forms a collection of ephemera that may have a value for scholars, such as books printed in Oldham during the nineteenth century or of Manchester theatre programmes.

In at least one instance the reason why a book-buyer did not read his books was that he had not yet learnt how to read. H. F. Stewart describes the activities of one small boy:

> He began collecting before he could read and he used to trot with his 1d. weekly pocket-money to the bookseller's, say, 'Book, please,' and go away hugging whatever scrapings of the press the shopman chose to bestow.[1]

The love of books remained, for the small boy was Edward Gordon Duff, who afterwards became an eminent bibliographer. Half a century later, in March 1925, his library was sold at Sotheby's for more than £8,000.

It is not only habitual book-buyers who have many books that they do not often read. Many houses have bookcases containing a set of leather-bound volumes because they look so handsome, a row of modern first editions because somebody has said that they will go up in price, a few school prizes and university textbooks preserved from inertia or for sentimental reasons, and a few Penguins for the owner to read.

Discussions of the reasons why people collect books often make the mistake of assuming that there is only a single reason. There are many, and a collector may be influenced by many different motives according to his mood. Book-collectors are too inclined to be on the defensive in giving their reasons for indulging in their hobby. They are like the stamp-collectors who say that they collect stamps because doing so teaches them such a lot about geography. The fact is that they collect stamps because they want to and that is sufficient reason. It is worthwhile to examine one's reasons for collecting books, not as a defence against a charge that no one

[1] H. F. Stewart, *Francis Jenkinson* (CUP, 1926), p. 30.

has any business to bring, but because to have a knowledge of the reasons for collecting is the best way of increasing the pleasure to be derived from the hobby.

It is necessary to distinguish between the book-buyer and the book-collector. The former includes the latter, but there are many book-buyers who possess thousands of volumes who cannot be regarded as collectors at all, and most of them have no wish to be so regarded.

At one time or another many men of letters have rhapsodized about the pleasures of reading and have vied with one another to find imagery adequate to apply to books. These rhapsodies tend to provoke a reaction, as when one academic man said of the Reading Room of the British Library:

> Isn't it wonderful to think of all those books, containing the best that has been known and thought in the world, the choice thoughts of the world's greatest men, and to know that you don't have to read any of them.

The last dozen words are mere academic flippancy. Scholars react against insincere enthusiasm by pretending to find learned works unattractive. A much-respected Professor of Theology once said that his wife was in the habit of reading detective stories in bed and sitting up half the night to find out who did it, whereas he took a theological treatise to bed and was asleep in five minutes.

In some families reading can arouse as much hostility as collecting. Those who take no pleasure in reading resent the competition for the attention of their families which books, like television, can provide. Robert Roberts, in his account of a working-class childhood in Salford, describes the anger which his father felt on finding one of his daughters reading:

> 'That child's fuddled with books!' my father complained 'She'll go funny!'
> Ellie looked up, smiling nervously.
> 'Leave her,' Mother told him. 'I was like that once.'

'Once! You're not much better now! I've come into this kitchen,' he fumed, 'and every living soul's been reading except the damned cat!'

Mother laughed. 'We'll have to do something about that cat!'[1]

Not everyone who is fond of reading is fond of buying books. Public libraries are so plentiful and efficient that it is possible to be an omnivorous reader while owning very few books oneself. The London Library, founded in 1841, has served the needs of many men of letters, including Carlyle, Dickens, Tennyson, Kipling and T. S. Eliot. When it was opened there were 3,000 books for its 500 members; now there are a million books for the 6,000 members. The subscription was at first a guinea but it is now £30, and Herculean efforts are needed to keep it down to that figure. Libraries are a perfectly adequate source for the supply of books that are to be read once and then forgotten, but there are many reasons why using a lending library is not enough. The chief of these is that lending libraries make inadequate provision for re-reading. The serious reader often wants to remind himself of something that he has come across in his reading, and even a frivolous book will stand re-reading after a time. The re-reading of such books is perhaps the best kind of bedtime reading because it is the least exacting. Fiction is not always the easiest genre to read. It calls for a sustained effort of attention to follow the plot, and a reader who is too tired to do this can derive more pleasure from reading snippets from a newspaper or an anecdotal biography. It is well to have more than one kind of book at hand to provide for varying needs. All readers of detective stories are liable to feel from time to time that they simply don't care who did it, and the next stage is to reflect that one might just as well be working or at least reading something with a bit more bite in it.

[1] Robert Roberts, *A Ragged Schooling* (Manchester University Press, 1976), p. 27.

There are other reasons why one cannot rely wholly on libraries. The book that we require may not be there when we want it and the library service which will order books in response to specific requests takes time. Then again, the distinction between books for reading and reference books is not clear-cut. When reading a book one often finds passages that one wants to mark for re-reading in certain specified circumstances. There is a lot to be said for borrowing a book in order to read it and then deciding whether it is worth buying.

There are, too, reference books which one frequently wants quickly, ranging from the *Oxford English Dictionary* or the *Dictionary of National Biography* to the Automobile Association's list of hotels. The decision to consult a particular book is more likely to be acted upon if the reader has the book on his own shelves than if he has to defer action until he is next in a library.

It must be admitted that there are dangers in excessive book-buying. It is possible to spend so much time in dipping into one's recent purchases and in reading a book because one has happened to come across a second-hand copy, that a well-planned programme of reading may suffer. There is also the danger of wasting time in reading out-of-date books, simply because one happens to have them.

Even if a book-buyer reads his books, he is in danger of confusing ends with means by becoming merely well-read. The well-read man's aim when he meets a man of similar tastes, is to get his victim into a corner to prove that he has read more than he has. Some readers are content to reflect for a long time over a small volume of aphorisms; others go in for quantity. William Beckford, the author of *Vathek*, felt that he must have something to read when passing through Lausanne, so he bought the library of Gibbon, who had lived there for some time. This was not merely a rich man's acquisitiveness, for Beckford shut himself up for six weeks, reading from early in the morning until night, and then leaving the library behind in Lausanne. The lust for quantity is liable to attack any book-buyer who has the means to gratify it. Richard Heber (1773–1833) owned 200,000 volumes and Charles Sarolea, who was Professor of French at Edinburgh in the early part of the present century, had more than half that number. His collection now forms part of the library of the University of Keele.

The inveterate reader is in danger of treating reading as a substitute for living. A cartoon by Clarence Day, the author of *Life with Father*, shows a number of boys swimming in a river while on the bank sits a bespectacled boy with a pile of books with such titles as *How to Swim* and *Lives of the Great Swimmers*. Fortunately, membership of this group of compulsive readers is not necessarily a life-membership. It is a stage through which most intelligent young people pass after they have first discovered the pleasures of reading. They dash eagerly from one book to another without pausing to digest what they have read. Their own writings are usually a mass of quotations citing authority for ideas which in a few years they will be willing to take for granted. Holbrook Jackson's *The Anatomy of Bibliomania* (Soncino Press, 1930) is a vast treasure-house of information and its author is obviously a very well-read man, but the book would have been better if it had been half the length and if many of the supporting opinions had been omitted. Can the author have had his tongue in cheek when, in the chapter 'Vain and Pedantic Reading Condemned', he protests against those who 'disport their secondhand stock of ideas and information' and on a single page quotes in his support Colton's *Lacon*, Crabbe, Montaigne, Samuel Butler, Kipling and Earle's *Microcosmography*? Quotations are useful only if they express an author's thoughts with a pungency to which he himself cannot attain, and the merely well-read man has been well described by Pope:

> The bookful blockhead, ignorantly read,
> With loads of learned lumber in his head.[1]

[1] *An Essay on Criticism*, 612 f.

What distinguishes a collector from a book-buyer is the element of excess in a controlled direction. The book-buyer buys books because he wants to read them, or thinks that he may want to do so some day. He is interested in all sorts of subjects and therefore the books that he buys tend to be miscellaneous. Within his chosen field the book-collector will buy more than he is ever likely to read. If he feels that the four folios of Shakespeare are necessary to his collection, he will not feel bound to read all four of them. He buys a book because it is necessary to fill a gap in a well-balanced collection on his chosen subject.

A collector will very rarely achieve his aim of completeness within a limited field, and if he does achieve it, the chances are that he will then lose interest in his collection. It is even more true of collecting than of most human activities that it is a better thing to travel hopefully than to arrive. One piece of information that a collector fortunately does not have at the outset is the high price that he will have to pay for each acquisition as his collection approaches completeness, but he would do well when choosing a field to make sure that the rarities that will be necessary to a complete collection are not so highly priced that he can never hope to buy them.

The most obvious satisfaction that a collector obtains is the gratification of his acquisitive instinct; but his pleasure goes much further than that. He derives satisfaction by bringing order out of chaos. A single volume, when it is part of a miscellaneous lot, may be unimportant, but it acquires significance if placed side by side with other books, and the book-collector enjoys exercising his judgement in deciding what these books are and his skill as a hunter in tracking them down. On the other hand a man may frequent second-hand book-shops for many years without building up a collection; it would be more true to say that a large accumulation of books has happened to him. Augustine Birrell expresses the point of view of the habitual book-buyer:

I confess to knowing one or two men . . . who, on the plea of being pressed with business, or because they were going to a funeral, have passed a bookshop in a strange town without so much as stepping inside 'just to see whether the fellow had anything'.[1]

It is a not uncommon pattern for a book-buyer gradually to become a collector when he has taken the edge off his appetite for buying the books that he wants to read. He does not stop buying books that lie outside the scope of his collection, but he builds up a special collection within a large accumulation. He often finds that he has acquired one or more embryo special collections simply by following his interests.

A collection can be formed without the owner having any interest in its subject, and many librarians build up special collections in this way, but the best collections are formed by book-buyers who have a passionate interest in the subject of the collection as well as knowledge, both general and specialized, and a mastery of techniques.

Sometimes a collector may himself use his books as the basis for scholarly work, as Michael Sadleir did in compiling his bibliography of nineteenth-century fiction on the basis of his own collection. More often his books will be used by somebody else, since the qualities necessary for a scholar and for a collector may not be found in the same man.

A good collector needs intelligence, pertinacity and money. If, as often happens, he has only the first two of these qualifications, he has to choose his collecting field with great care in order to avoid the fields where a single purchase might cost more than he will be able to spend on books in the whole of his lifetime. He learns by experience, and consequently every collector should be prepared to sell as well as to buy. The most common mistake made by the beginner is not to recognize the importance of condition, and he must be prepared to get rid of his cheap imperfect copies when he finds the good copies that he would have been wiser to wait for in the first instance. It is best not to begin by buying expensive books,

[1] *Collected Essays and Addresses* (Dent, 1922), III.77.

however highly recommended; in this way the collector can ensure that his mistakes do not cost him very much.

Societies of book-collectors can serve a very useful function in the sharing of experience. A collector can take warning from the mistakes of others as well as those that he makes himself. Many of the important questions that he has to answer are questions of opinion, not of fact, and it is useful to check one's own opinions and those of others as widely as possible. Matters that can be learnt by conversation with other collectors or booksellers include questions of price or rarity, opinions about the reliability of a particular bookseller and information about which booksellers are the most likely to stock a particular type of book.

The collector who reads his books will be happier than the one who doesn't, though a lot will depend on the subject. Some collections require a long purse but little knowledge, and the wealthy collector will concentrate on acquiring 'high spots'. Some collectors buy not only to read but also to write other books, and Gibbon's account of the younger Gordian (d. A.D. 237) shows that he thought highly of this type of collector:

> Twenty-two acknowledged concubines, and a library of sixty-two thousand volumes, attested the variety of his inclinations, and from the productions which he left behind him, it appears that the former as well as the latter were designed for use rather than ostentation.[1]

A collector who does not read his collection may still be performing a very useful service for his fellowmen. He is particularly useful if he chooses to collect books of no very obvious value, in that he may preserve from oblivion or destruction books that other people without the acquisitive instinct will be very glad to read.

A collector who does not read his collection may still be per-

---

[1] Gibbon's *Decline and Fall of the Roman Empire*, 'Everyman' edn., vol. 1, p. 171.

the one who follows well-trodden paths – such a collector simply pushes up prices – but he is the man who strikes out on new ones. He anticipates the fields which will be useful to the historian or the scholar of the future, and his reward is that, until he becomes well-known as a collector, he buys his books cheaply.

Anyone who buys a lot of books is liable to acquire some duplicates, and with some extremists this is a deliberate policy. Richard Heber is said to have maintained that a collector needs three copies of every book in his possession: one for his library, one to read and one to lend to his friends. In the less opulent conditions of today, this is too ambitious an aim. A collector need not be ashamed of possessing three editions of a book, but not all his books need to be in all three categories. Public libraries now make provision for book-borrowers, and the three copies that a collector of today might wish to possess of some of his books are the first edition, a library edition competently edited with large type and broad margins, and a pocket edition for reading in bed.

The accumulation of duplicates by wealthy collectors can reach a point hard to defend. The argument for holding duplicates of older books is that a good deal of serious research takes the form of comparing superficially identical copies of a book, finding that they are not identical, and drawing conclusions from the differences. It is a difficult question to decide what is a duplicate. It was once absurdly suggested that a library with a large collection of Caxtons should sell most of them on the grounds that one Caxton is enough for any library. For the specialist the existence of many books in one limited category in a single building is a great advantage.

In defence of collectors one should say that it is by their zeal and expert knowledge that large quantities of ephemera are preserved at all. The collector who performs this service is not the wealthy collector of first folios or private press books; these are so obviously attractive that they are in little danger of accidental destruction. It is rather the man with a knowledge of the history of book-collecting, who knows which books have become scarce in the past and who can look ahead to forecast which books, plentiful today, will be scarce in the future. Collections of this kind are Michael Sadleir's three-deckers now in the Library of the University of California at Los Angeles, and George Thomason's Civil War tracts in the British Library.

Those who deride book-collectors make great play with the difference that an apparently unimportant detail can make to the price of a book. This is simply a matter of supply and demand. Naturally a perfect copy will be worth more than an imperfect one. How much more it is worth will depend on the number of people who attach importance to the difference and on the length of their purses. There is here some consolation for the impecunious book-collector. If the presence of half-titles and original boards is going to increase the value of a book tenfold, let him leave the acquisition of perfect copies to the man who can afford the luxury while he concentrates on building up a collection of copies without half-titles or the prized 'blank leaf at end', but with the text sound and complete. Similarly there is consolation to be derived from the fashions in book-collecting. So long as the attention of wealthy collectors is concentrated on colour-plate books, the prices of other books are more likely to remain at a reasonable level.

There is an analogy between the buying of books and the acquisition of material wealth. The ideas that you can keep in your head correspond to the small change that you can keep in your pocket; those that you can obtain from the books on your shelves correspond to the money that you have in the bank; and the ideas that you can obtain from the books in a public library correspond to investments in property or equities. They may be very valuable but you can't always get at them just when you want them.

The book-collector is concerned to bring the right book to the right place at the right time. If books remained in print for ever and if booksellers always had well-stocked shops or an efficient system of ordering books and getting hold of them promptly, there would be less point in collecting them. Unfortunately most books are out of print, and the cost to a bookseller of stocking all the books that are in print would completely swallow his meagre profits. Those profits would be even more meagre if he were to develop an efficient system of informing his customers when a book was likely to go out of print, for one of the motives that induce a potential reader to buy a book is the realization that it may not be available when he actually wants to read it. Just as the manufacturers of mustard are said to make their profit from what is left on the side of the plate, so publishers and booksellers, especially of books in series, make their profit from the books that people buy in the hope that they may have time to read them one day. The same is true of books bought by libraries. Those who are responsible for the allocation of funds to libraries sometimes point out indignantly that expensive books may remain on library shelves for decades without ever being consulted. This is not a good reason why they should not be bought. It is the business of a library to provide a copy of a book in its field when that book is needed and, once the book has been allowed to go out of print, it is usually too late to buy a copy. In fact, if libraries were to observe a more cautious policy in buying little-used books, many of these books could never be published at all. It is a well known fact of publishing economics that by far the biggest element in the cost of printing a book is the cost of setting up the type. By buying a book that will be little used a library is making its contribution to the cost of publication. Without that contribution from a large number of libraries, the cost of an important scholarly book might be ten times its present price. There is room for yet more experiment in the method of reproduction of books. With the spread of photographic methods it is possible to reproduce scholarly books in small editions at much lower prices than those involved when a book is set up from type. But here book-buyers must depend on the co-operation of publishers.

Authors would like a lot of people to buy and read their books; they are dissatisfied on both counts. Even people who

think of themselves as bookish will not always include purchase as one of the possible ways of acquiring a book. A quite
eminent scholar boasted of having written to the author of a
newly-published book to ask where it could be obtained and
added 'And, do you know, he *sent* me a copy'. A less generous
author would have replied 'From a bookseller'. The failure of
the public to read newly-published books is something that
authors learn to live with, although the comments of their
friends sometimes turn the knife in the wound. When
William Henry, Duke of Gloucester, said 'Another damned,
thick, square book! Always scribble, scribble, scribble! Eh!
Mr Gibbon?' he no doubt felt that he was giving a friendly
reception to *The Decline and Fall of the Roman Empire*. Mr
Casaubon, in *Middlemarch*, 'suspected the Archdeacon of not
having read' his pamphlets (ch. 29), and another author complained that people made a point of not buying his books.
Authors who are wise do not ask for their own books in
bookshops. A *New Yorker* cartoon showed an angry-looking
middle-aged man saying to a frightened assistant in a bookshop: 'You're darn right I'm certain such an author exists.'

If book-collectors are inclined to get uppish, it is well to
look for a moment at the Seven Deadly Sins in relation to
book-collecting. The chief of them is Pride, and is there any
collector who can say that he is not proud of his collection?
Then there is Avarice. Well, avarice is the whole point of
collecting: the collector hoards books as the miser hoards
gold. And his activities are not far removed from Gluttony:
the glutton demands an excess of food for the body whereas
the book-collector demands an excess of food for the mind.
Wrath is the sin that you indulge in when the book for which
you have sent in a bid at an auction sale is knocked down to a
higher bidder. As for Envy, I indulge in that sin freely whenever I see the books of another collector. It may seem that the
book-collector is not guilty of Luxuria, or Lust, but many
collectors are attracted by the large class of books which the
Bodleian Library, permitting itself an erudite pun, classifies
under the Greek letter *phi* or which booksellers describe as

'curious' and keep on a shelf well within their line of vision. As for Accidie or Sloth, what else is it that causes a collector to refuse to dust his books? We can only hope that book-collecting may act as a sublimation of these various undesirable impulses. If we did not collect books we might be doing something else even more socially reprehensible. One sin that a book-collector can commit, though I don't think that many do, is to spend more money than he can afford on books.

Pleasure is mixed with pain. Edmund Gosse was once outbid by Lord Rosebery at a book-auction. He sought comfort from a friendly bookseller, saying: 'He gets everything; he was born to get everything.' The bookseller replied: 'No, not everything. He has not, and never will have, the exquisite pleasure of buying what he knows he cannot afford.'[1]

Augustine Birrell once said that it is as absurd to be proud of having two thousand books as it is to be proud of having two overcoats. He suggested that ten thousand books was a nice figure to aim at. There may seem to be no particular point in counting them, and, when you are planning a library, the yard is a more convenient unit of measurement than the book, but to use it seems disrespectful. If you ever make an insurance claim, however, it will be useful to be able to state the approximate number of books in various categories.

There is no particular virtue in large numbers of books. If the collector's interests are specialized, large numbers are unnecessary, and if they range widely, large numbers can be a nuisance when he is moving house; they can often dictate what kind of house he lives in. I have from time to time employed removal contractors to move large numbers of books, and I found their comments very interesting. Four of the men on one job reminded me of the supernatural spirits in Hardy's *The Dynasts*. They gazed at the books silently for a few minutes; then one, the Spirit Ironic, said 'Have all these to go to a private house?' The realist then asked an important question: 'Upstairs or downstairs?' In the mean-

[1] E. H. M. Cox, ed., *The Library of Edmund Gosse*, Dulau 1924, p. xxii.

time, the Spirit of the Pities had been examining the shelves and said in an awed voice: 'Have you seen, Bill? Double rows.' They spent a day on the job and, towards the end of the day, one of the men asked Bill if he was going out that evening. His reply was 'No, I think I'll curl up with a nice book.' Another comment was that of a cheerful Cockney who was delivering a heavy bookcase. He carried it on his shoulder up a hill because it wasn't worth while bringing the lorry, and when he saw that the house contained a number of similar bookcases, he asked, with interest, 'What is this? A nobby?'

CHAPTER II

WHAT TO COLLECT

THERE is no doubt that Charles Lamb was a book-lover. In his 'Detached Thoughts on Books and Reading' in *The Last Essays of Elia* he declares that he has no repugnances and that he can read anything which he can call a book. He then makes his famous distinction between real books and books which are no books:

> In this catalogue of books which are no books – biblia a-biblia – I reckon Court Calendars, Directories, Pocket Books, Draught Boards, bound and lettered on the back, Scientific Treatises, Almanacks, Statutes at Large; the works of Hume, Gibbon, Robertson, Beattie, Soame Jenyns, and, generally all those volumes which no gentleman's library should be without! the Histories of Flavius Josephus (that learned Jew), and Paley's Moral Philosophy. With those exceptions, I can read almost anything. I bless my stars for a taste so catholic, so unexcluding.

The inclusion of Gibbon in this list can best be described as a piece of cheek. Those collectors whose interest in the history of science has pushed the prices of scientific treatises up to dizzy heights might feel some resentment at the inclusion of this category, but it could be replied that Lamb is speaking of reading, not of collecting. Lamb shares the collector's interest in the physical shape and binding of a book, but he is no collector. He makes the commonsense point that not all books deserve a magnificent binding, but he reveals his lack of sympathy with a true collector by a parenthesis which he slips into his declaration: 'A Shakespeare or a Milton (unless the

first edition), it were mere foppery to trick out in gay apparel.'
Anyone fortunate enough to possess a first edition of
Shakespeare or Milton would be well advised to leave it
alone instead of providing it with a magnificent binding.

From the earliest days of collecting there has been a good
deal of variety about the various categories of books which
appeal to collectors. In *The Rambler* (No 177, 1751) Dr
Johnson includes a satirical description of a coffee-house literary society. Hirsutus collected black-letter books and was able
to show the deficiencies of the best catalogues. Chartophylus
was trying to complete a series of gazettes and succeeded, his
last acquisition being wrapped round a tin of tobacco. Others
collected neglected pamphlets or a letter written in the reign
of Elizabeth. Johnson thought all this a waste of time and said
that the collectors should have helped the advancement of
human knowledge instead of being 'diverted by minute
emulation and laborious trifles'. But what is useful knowledge? Johnson admitted that any occupation that is not
positively vicious helps to keep a man out of idleness and vice,
and book-collecting may be tolerated if only for this modest
reason.

The number of books in existence is so large that in order to
carve out a manageable field for a collection that is to approach
anywhere near completeness considerable subdivision is
necessary. The collector who chooses as his field illustrated
books or drama may bring together a large number of books,
but there will be enormous gaps. If he is to avoid such gaps,
he has to limit his field, say to English illustrated books of a
single decade or the plays of a single dramatist, since a large
part of the interest in collecting springs from the discovery
of ancillary material that illustrates a subject that at first seems
barren.

Specialization may be topographical; a man whose work
takes him some distance from his native county may find his
homesickness assuaged by the building up of a county collection. It may be biographical; an author collection is the most
common kind of literary collection, but also one can

choose a genre collection, such as the Edwardian novel or the poetry of the First World War. It is possible to specialize on some aspect of social history; one collector decided to concentrate on the history of coffee-drinking in England. It may be that the unifying theme of a collection is not concerned with subject matter; it may be the work of a particular printer or publisher, especially if the printer is an innovator or the publisher a man whose productions follow a homogeneous plan. Some collectors in their quest for rarity have confined their collecting to books which they believed to be unique. Collecting on these lines produces a miscellaneous heap of books of little interest with perhaps a few important rarities among them. A book may be rare because of its unimportance, and there is always the chance that a previously unnoticed copy will turn up. It is even possible to specialize in forgeries; the Wise forgeries have a place in the history of publishing and they attract many collectors (see Chapter VIII).

The value of a well-planned collection is greater than the sum of its parts, and this is true whether we regard 'value' as meaning either usefulness or monetary value. In any worthwhile collection completeness is unattainable, but a collector may reach the point at which the books that he needs to fill the gaps are so scarce that they may never turn up in his lifetime. How is he to occupy the fifteen or twenty years that may elapse before the book that he wants comes on the market? It is at this point that he may realize that it is time to choose another subject. A collector can never be confident that price movements will always be upwards, but when he reaches such rarefied fields the element of uncertainty is greater than usual. If a book comes on the market only once in every ten years or so, its price is likely to depend on a number of accidents, such as the survival with undiminished enthusiasm of two collectors with deep pockets. If one of them dies, the price may fall into the basement.

A collector must specialize to save himself from the two evils of excessive outlay and an excessive number of books.

This advice is given to collectors by most writers on the subject, including booksellers, who show their self-denial in giving this advice, because the failure to specialize, against which they warn the collector, is the quality which makes the collector a good customer.

In the choice of a field there are two extremes to be avoided. The first is the field so popular that prices are high and rarities virtually unobtainable because other collectors have got in first. The other extreme is one so unexplored that nobody but the collector takes any interest in it. Books in such a field are hard to buy because no bookseller thinks it worth his while to stock them, and when the collection is formed, it is unsaleable. Choice of field involves timing: the successful collector is one who gets in early in a field not yet popular but about to become so.

Completeness within a chosen field is the aim of most collectors. In choosing a subject for specialization, the first thing to look for is the price of the rarest books in that field. If they are very expensive or, as sometimes happens, unobtainable because the few existing copies are in public libraries, the ordinary collector will have to choose another subject.

Familiarity with a large public library or even with the stock of a dealer in rare books can easily fill a private collector with despair. When confronted with a thousand books, each one of which is worth more than he can ever hope to spend on his entire library, the collector may say 'What's the use?' The remedy for this mood is a wise choice of field. Caxtons are not for him but, for the present at least, the bibliophile may be able to think of a collection of Victorian three-decker novels. In course of time these too may be out of reach of all but the rich collector, but by then other fields will have been opened up. If Victorian novels do not appeal to him or if they are already beyond his reach, what about a collection of Penguins?

Some collectors fix a period and confine themselves to books within that period. Others fix a limit of price. One collector claimed that his limit was fourpence, but that was last century.

Fashions in book-collecting tend to follow fashions in education. When English education was in the main based on the classics, people collected them. Elizabethan plays were rediscovered at the beginning of the nineteenth century and the Romantic poets at the end. One development since the Second World War has been the greater attention paid to first editions of books dealing with science and economics.

Collectors who do not trust their own judgement clutch avidly at lists that are offered to them from time to time by writers on book-collecting, bearing such titles as 'The Hundred Best Novels'. Such lists appeal to the love of completeness which is strong in collectors, but others find that the exercise of their own judgement in forming a specialized collection is part of the fascination of collecting.

The easiest kind of specialized collection is the author collection. A prolific or well-known author can make heavy demands on a collector in both space and money. Desmond Flower's collection of Voltaire ran to 1350 volumes and was sold to the bookseller El Dieff for £24,000. There are thus obvious advantages in collecting an unpopular author. On the other hand, it can be discouraging. John Carter wrote:

> Bibliophily in its broader aspects is a sociable and an emulative pursuit, and many a promising special line has gone sour on the collector himself because his interest could not survive the profound and persistent disinterest of his fellow-collectors.[1]

The most important thing is to choose an author who, whether popular or not, appeals to the collector himself. Once this requirement is satisfied, the far-seeing but impoverished collector will do well to concentrate on authors who, for one reason or another, are undervalued. If he can find them, he will seek out the works of authors whose reputation is moving upwards. He will do well to collect the work of

[1] *Taste and Technique in Book-Collecting* (CUP, 1948), p. 89.

authors of the second rank, not too prolific, authors that future readers will not willingly ignore but whose works are not likely to be reprinted in full. There are some major novelists, such as George Gissing or Anthony Trollope, who may satisfy this requirement. Attempts to reprint the whole of Trollope have so far been unsuccessful, in spite of his popularity. The effort may yet be successful, but there are many Victorian novels, such as those of Anthony's brother Thomas Adolphus, that are elusive and not likely to be reprinted.

A book-buyer who tries to build up a complete author collection has special difficulty if his author is one who thinks that nobody minds his books being all of different kinds, because the books on subjects remote from the author's usual field tend to be unexpectedly hard to find. Most books are rare, except for those published in a series of cheap reprints, but their rarity passes unnoticed because nobody wants them. If the accident that the author has published books in a quite different field makes him a 'collected author', a book of specialized interest with only a small printing may become eagerly sought after. The novels of Ernest Bramah have quite a strong appeal for many readers, but devotees of Kai Lung may have difficulty in finding *The Eyes of Max Carrados* or *A Servant of the State* and even greater difficulty in finding *English Copper Coins* or *English Farming and Why I Turned It Up*. Some collectors meet the difficulty by restricting themselves to one particular aspect of an author's work. It is possible to collect Lewis Carroll without touching the mathematical works of C. L. Dodgson, and the collector of Kingsley's novels need not feel bound to acquire *What Then Does Dr Newman Mean?* It is to be hoped that collectors will not regard off-subject books as a suitable field for collecting; if they do, such books will become rarer still.

A book may also be unexpectedly rare because it lies at the intersection of two or more currents of demand. If a novelist, popular with collectors, writes a book on cricket illustrated by a well-known book-illustrator, the book will be in demand by three different sets of collectors, and the demand will be reflected in the price.

The collector of authors like G. K. Chesterton and E. V. Lucas, who have combined the careers of novelist and journalist, has the problem that many of their first editions were issued in periodicals; but a number of collectors acquire the writings of journalists when published as books without feeling obliged to take an interest in the real first edition of their work in periodicals.

The love of completeness is liable to be exploited by publishers. If an author, alive or dead, is widely collected, there will soon appear little brochures of fragments of the sweepings from his desk, published in limited editions at high prices. Since these fragments have not been published before, they are first editions and so earn a place in bibliographies and on the collectors' lists of desiderata.

Great libraries like the Bodleian have in the past neglected ephemera, but today minor poets and novelists are encouraged to clean out their desks by the high prices that libraries will pay for manuscripts and early drafts.

An author collection becomes more interesting and varied when the collector decides to include *ana*, material about an author as distinct from material by him. Every inclusion involves the exercise of personal judgement by the collector and the result may be either brilliant or disastrous, but here completeness ceases to be an important aim. Such a collection could include all books dedicated to his author and books which obviously influenced him. Such a book as *Select Poems of William Barnes* (London, 1908) might claim to be more than *ana* in a Hardy collection, since it has a preface and notes on words by Hardy himself. Another extension of an author collection is that of anthologies containing a few poems by the author collected. Another, to which limits of some kind must be fixed, is that of books by and about an author's friends which make some reference to the collected author. Most nineteenth-century literary biographies will include references to authors such as Dickens.

Some books acquire an added value from having passed through the hands of a famous collector; scientific books acquire added value when they have once been the property of another eminent scientist, especially if he has annotated them.

A field that is ignored by most collectors, though it makes a strong appeal to a few, is that of manuscripts. The uniqueness of manuscripts introduces a new problem for the collector: the manuscripts that he acquires may be important to scholars engaged in literary or historical research. Is the collector to refuse access to his manuscripts from a fear that publication may lessen their value or is he to accept appointment as an unpaid librarian, which may make heavy demands on his time? Newspapers sometimes print letters from research workers asking for the loan of manuscripts, but there is some reason to believe that one purpose of such letters is to warn other researchers that a book on the subject is in preparation. Problems of custody and access weigh most heavily on the owners of stately homes who have inherited large collections without much interest in their contents. This is the plight of the fictional Lord Ampersand in Michael Innes's *The Ampersand Papers* (1978):

> Lord Ampersand began to receive letters from members of the investigating class – most of them with American addresses – the general tenor of which was that his family had lately been discovered to merit regard. So would he kindly answer this question and that – and could he undertake to be at home in his ancestral seat or stately residence throughout the month of August, during which the writer would be vacationing in England.

To every problem there is a solution, though that adopted by Lord Ampersand might not commend itself to everybody:

> Lord Ampersand takes pleasure in intimating that the Muniment Room at Treskinnick Castle will in future be open on the

33

first Thursday of every month between the hours of two and
five of the clock in the afternoon
Railway station: Lesnewth: 15 miles

(Chapter 1)

The best solution is probably to lend the manuscripts for a
limited period to a public library, which will allow scholars to
consult them under supervision.

Medieval manuscripts were often created as works of art to
be admired for their beauty and in such manuscripts one
sometimes suspects that mistakes were left uncorrected because alterations would spoil the appearance of the page.
They are the medieval equivalents of our modern private
press books. An author's manuscripts, on the other hand, are
most interesting when they are least beautiful, that is when
they show many corrections. The illustrations in older manuscripts have two kinds of interest apart from their literary
interest: artistic and documentary, in their portrayal of contemporary social life, costumes and architecture.

E. P. Goldschmidt said, as the result of long experience:

The market value of medieval manuscripts [. . .] is quite independent of their contents. It is determined solely by the dominant
question: are there any pictures in them?[1]

He goes on to say that the high prices sometimes paid for
manuscripts are in no way connected with their being books:
'They are regarded as book-shaped *objets d'art* which contain painted pictures.'

Medieval booksellers ('stationers') provided textbooks for
students. Their main source of income was not the selling of
books outright; it was the lending of books to allow copies to
be made of them and for this they were allowed to make a
charge which varied with the number of pages. They also
acted as pawnbrokers. Students pledged their books to the
'librarii' of the university and such loans are recorded in the

[1] In *Talks on Book-Collecting*, ed. P. H. Muir (Cassell, 1952), p. 25.

covers of old manuscripts. Other booksellers were purveyors of fashionable reading matter to the nobility and gentry. This was the trade that Caxton took up with printed books. Others supplied prayer-books to the clergy and reference books to lawyers and physicians.

The great attraction of the collection of manuscripts is that every manuscript is unique. It would seem, therefore, that book-collectors, who value rarity, would greatly value manuscripts, each of which represents rarity in its highest obtainable form, but for some reason they don't. One reason for the neglect of manuscripts is no doubt that their very uniqueness makes them difficult to value. A collector likes to think that, in case of need, he can sell his collection for a price of which he can make a rough estimate, based on the prices at which identical copies have been bought and sold, but the collector of manuscripts has no such easy guide. Medieval illuminated manuscripts sell for very high prices, but there are not many of these left to come on the market. Later manuscripts may still be expensive, but they offer scope to a collector who prefers to have a small collection and who enjoys the research involved in finding out as much as he can about his purchases.

Many of the later manuscripts that do come on the market are wills or deeds concerned with the transfer of property, but a number of them are letters. Collectors of manuscripts are likely to come into conflict with the collectors of autographs, because their needs are different. Modern collectors are generally wise enough to keep letters intact, but an earlier generation has left many fragments from which they have cut the signatures, thus earning the maledictions of their successors. It is desirable to collect a letter whose subject matter has some interest. The majority of letters that are offered for sale in lots are from people of some importance in their day but of little importance in ours; they are simply social notes declining invitations to dinner. The letters which are most worth collecting are those in which an author mentions historic events or a book written by himself or somebody else. An autograph letter becomes more interesting when it throws light on the personality of the writer. A letter by the undistinguished Poet Laureate Alfred Austin is a reply to a request for his autograph: 'It is my custom to ask all those who apply for my autograph and who can afford to do so, to send me one shilling (in stamps) in aid of my "Literary Charities".'

A letter may become valuable for accidental reasons. A signature much coveted by American collectors is that of Button Gwinnett of Georgia, one of the signatories of the Declaration of Independence. Many collectors try to bring together a letter from each of the signatories but Button Gwinnett's signature is rare because he was killed in a duel in 1777 while he was still young. The bookseller Rosenbach once paid $51,000 for a document bearing Gwinnett's signature.

Another kind of manuscript that can occasionally be found, often in an unexpected place, is the commonplace book. Readers would transcribe passages that specially appealed to them, and these passages might be interspersed with recipes or devotional material. Many medieval manuscripts were of this kind. At a time when manuscripts were few and expensive, a student might find it convenient to write his own library, and students of today find it convenient to supplement printed books with manuscript notes. In ancient Rome manuscripts were sometimes produced by dictation to a group of slaves, who thus produced multiple copies at little cost. Students of today, taking down notes at lectures, probably think that the practice is not obsolete.

It is clear that manuscripts cover a wide field ranging from priceless medieval manuscripts to social notes from one nonentity to another; perhaps the most interesting field for a collector is that consisting of the original manuscripts of literary works. The fair copy of one of his poems which T. S. Eliot wrote out for sale to benefit the funds of the London Library has less interest than a manuscript or a set of corrected proofs on which he recorded his second or third thoughts, even though these corrections may spoil the appearance of the manuscript. It is worth knowing whether an author wrote fluently and with ease or whether he struggled to find the exact word. John Heming and Henry Condell recorded in the prefatory matter to the First Folio of Shakespeare (1623): 'And what he thought, he uttered with that easiness, that we have scarce received from him a blot on his papers.'

The value of authors' drafts is beginning to be recognized, and perhaps exaggerated, when university libraries compete with one another to buy the rejected typescripts of minor authors. In the past, authors' original manuscripts were little valued and it is probable that rich stores of autograph letters and other material by nineteenth-century authors could be found among the archives of major publishers. Thomas Hardy gave many of his manuscripts away and, when he heard that the manuscript of one of his novels had been sold at a high price, he made the wry comment: 'If I'd known it would fetch so much, I'd have used better paper.'

Private press publications set out to achieve a high standard of book-production and it is therefore natural that they should appeal to collectors. By the middle of the nineteenth century the standard of book-design and printing had sunk to a low level, and reform came from the private press movement, which has had a strong influence on modern publishing design. A private press is not easy to define. C. R. Ashbee, who founded the Essex House Press, attempted the task of definition in 1909. He said that a private press was

> a Press whose objective is first of all an aesthetic one, a Press that if it is to have real worth challenges support on a basis of standard, caters for a limited market, and is not concerned with the question of commercial development of printing by machinery.[1]

[1] C. R. Ashbee, 'The Essex House Press: and the Purpose or Meaning of a Private Press', *The Book Collector's Quarterly* No. XI, July–September, 1933, p. 72.

This definition will serve as a general description of private press publications with its stress on quality and the appeal to a limited public, but it has to be interpreted loosely to avoid excluding such a press as the Nonesuch press, which employed commercial printers and published some books in unlimited editions.

The private press movement owed much of its impetus to William Morris, but book-production was only one of his many interests. Soon after his marriage he built Red House at Upton in Kent and was repelled by the poor quality of the goods available for furnishing and decorating his home; he therefore designed his own furniture, wallpaper and fabrics. He was a man of strong passions and once, when he found an example of church-restoration that he particularly disliked, he stamped up and down the nave, waving his arms above his head and bellowing, 'The pigs, the swine, God DAMN their souls'.[1] Morris had always admired the calligraphy of the Middle Ages and the early printing which took its place, and in the publications of the Kelmscott Press, which he founded at Hammersmith in 1890, he aimed at producing books in the same tradition which it would be a pleasure to look at as examples of printing and arrangement of type. His original intention was to print only a few copies of each book for presentation to his friends, but popular demand led him to print a few hundred copies of each title for sale. Morris designed founts of type and ornamental letters and borders for the Kelmscott Press, from which fifty-three books were issued, including several of Morris's own works and reprints of English classics, especially those with a medieval interest. His masterpiece was the Kelmscott Chaucer, completed in June 1896. A feature of the books of this Press is the contrast between the rich black type and the gleaming white paper, a great improvement on the grey effect of much late Victorian

---

[1] Alan G. Thomas, *Great Books and Book Collectors* (Weidenfeld & Nicolson, 1975), p. 215.

printing. Another is Morris's conception of the double opening, not the single page, as the unit of design. The decoration
is too exuberant for many people today, but we can appreciate
Morris's insistence on the use of the finest materials, such as
hand-made paper.

The influence of Morris is to be found in the work of
Charles Robert Ashbee (1863–1942), an architect and craftsman who in 1888 established the Guild of Handicraft in
Commercial Street, London, and in 1891 moved to Essex
House, Mile End Road. In 1902 he moved the Guild, number-
ing 150 members, to Chipping Campden in Gloucestershire,
where it remained until it was wound up in 1907. Ashbee and
his friends practised furniture making and other crafts, but
their chief interest was in printing and bookbinding. He
bought Morris's two presses and employed three of his workmen. At the Essex House Press he printed eighty-seven items,
of which fifty-nine were books. He held that good typography and book-production were important but that the life
of the workshop came first.

Ashbee was disappointed in the results of his work as a
printer and he was resentful of the part played by commercial
printers.

> What we failed to understand was . . . that ultimately 'the
> Trade', seeing there was money in it, would set up sham
> presses to catch that money. And that is the reason why a
> hundred and one petty publishing firms have, since the nine-
> ties, called themselves 'presses'.[1]

The choice of books was more limited than that of the other
private presses. Ashbee was concerned chiefly with books
dealing with the crafts that he practised, with religion and
with 'higher education', as he understood the term, to include
a synthesis of Puritanism and Humanism.

[1] C. R. Ashbee, op. cit., p. 73.

Morris's ideals of craftsmanship were shared too by Thomas James Cobden-Sanderson (1840–1922), who had been a barrister but who retired from the bar in 1881 in order to work with his hands. Four years after Morris's death in 1896 Cobden-Sanderson joined with Emery Walker to found the Doves Press. He relied on beautiful type and the balance of the pages rather than decoration, and in contrast with the exuberance of Kelmscott books, the publications of the Doves Press showed a classic restraint. The masterpiece of the Press was the Doves Bible (1903–5) in five folio volumes.

In 1909 Cobden-Sanderson and Emery Walker quarrelled, but Cobden-Sanderson continued to print alone until 1916 and in the following year, in defiance of an agreement that he had made that the type should pass after his death to Emery Walker, he pitched the whole lot over Hammersmith Bridge into the Thames.

Another private press established under the influence of Morris was the Ashendene Press, founded by C. H. St John Hornby in 1895. Helped by his family, he began printing in a summer-house at Ashendene in Hertfordshire, but in 1899 he moved to Shelley House on the Chelsea Embankment. His first big book was a folio Dante, published in 1909, and among the last were the *Ecclesiasticus* (1932) and a *Descriptive Bibliography of Books Printed at the Ashendene Press* (1935). The Press remained in existence for forty years and printed about forty books.

The Golden Cockerel Press was founded by Harold Taylor in 1920 and it has had several owners. Its best work was the result of collaboration between Robert Gibbings, who became its owner in 1924, and Eric Gill. Their masterpiece was *The Four Gospels*, which showed harmony between the type and the wood-engravings with which Gill reproduced the opening words of each chapter, filling the spaces in the lettering with stylized figures. At Gill's suggestion the lines of prose were not 'justified' to achieve a straight right-hand margin, as in most printed books, because he thought it important to keep even spaces between the words, the usual way of avoiding a ragged right-hand margin being to vary the spaces between the words.

The Nonesuch Press, founded by Francis and Vera Meynell in 1923, showed a new conception of the private press. Hitherto every process had been carried out by hand, the founts of type were privately owned, and each edition was limited to about three hundred copies. Meynell used machine printing and employed commercial printers to issue much larger editions. In its first hundred publications the Nonesuch Press used nineteen different printers and twenty-six different type-faces. In the first prospectus Meynell declared his aims to be significance of subject, beauty and low price. His Press covered a wide range but it was especially strong in editions of books published in the seventeenth century, including the plays of Dryden, Congreve, Wycherley and Vanbrugh. Perhaps its most impressive publication was the edition of the works of Dickens, published in twenty-three volumes in 1938, which now sells for more than £1,000. The plates and blocks used for the original publications were bought from Dickens's publishers, Chapman & Hall, and one block was included with each set of the Works.

The willingness of the Nonesuch Press to co-operate with commercial printers had good results. It helped to remove the reproach that private presses were interested only in the wealthy collector and it strengthened the beneficent influence that private presses were having on book production in general, because the employment of commercial printers was not allowed to involve any relaxation of standards.

The books published in unlimited editions by the Nonesuch Press are well worth the attention of the book-collector. The volumes in 'The Nonesuch Library' were miracles of cheapness, each consisting of nearly a thousand pages and published for the most part at 10s 6d or 12s 6d. The volume devoted to Blake includes his complete poetry and prose, but with more prolific authors the pattern was an edited text of the writer's chief work with selections from his lesser writings and letters.

Among the authors included were Milton, Coleridge, Hazlitt, Lewis Carroll, Walt Whitman and Pushkin.

The number of private presses has increased to such an extent that some booksellers devote catalogues entirely to their publications. Out of the large number of books mention may be made of the Shakespeare Head Press editions of the eighteenth-century novelists Defoe, Fielding, Sterne, Smollett and Richardson, published between 1926 and 1931. These were limited to about 700 or 800 copies and printed in large type on excellent paper. The publishers made no attempt to compress a long novel into a single volume; *Tom Jones*, for example, is in four volumes. The books are convenient to handle and help to free private press publications from the reproach that they are handsome works of art rather than books to read.

The handsome appearance of private press books ensures that few copies are destroyed; they are expensive but not necessarily rare and do not need to be snapped up as soon as they are found on the grounds that they may never be seen again. The collector can usually be sure that they will be seen – at a price.

For the last two centuries the novel has been the predominant literary form in England and it therefore opens up a promising field for the collector who chooses a subdivision of manageable size.

In the latter part of the eighteenth century circulating libraries had become popular and publishers, assuming that the libraries would result in a reduction in sales, raised the prices of novels. The higher prices encouraged a still greater use of circulating libraries and the standard price of a three-volume novel became a guinea and a half. There were various attempts to break away from high prices and library control, such as the publication of cheap monthly parts and discount bookselling. But during the period of domination by the circulating libraries, nearly all sales of novels were to libraries, which often stuck their labels on the outside covers of novels.

A collector of three-deckers greatly limits his field if he refuses to buy ex-library copies. The stranglehold of the libraries was broken by George Moore. Mudie's Lending Library refused to circulate *A Modern Lover* because it was thought to be immoral and Moore published his next novel, *A Mummer's Wife*, and all his subsequent novels in one-volume editions.

In the early nineteenth century the cheap part-issue was not highly regarded and such esteem as it had came chiefly from the illustrations. The success of *Pickwick Papers* changed the status of the part issue for the next fifty years. Dickens had been commissioned by Chapman & Hall to fill out with text the plates which they had commissioned from Robert Seymour in 1836, and the book had an outstanding success. The part issue was used for books by Dickens, Thackeray, Ainsworth, Marryat, Trollope, and many other novelists. Parts were published monthly at a shilling; they were not liable to stamp duty and they made it possible for the middle classes to buy novels instead of borrowing the expensive three-deckers from circulating libraries. They competed with magazines and brought down the prices of magazines. This reduction adversely affected the sale of the competing part-issues. Dickens played a further role in widening the market for fiction when he founded *Household Words* in 1849 as a two-penny weekly. It ran *Cranford* (1851–3) and many of Dickens's own novels. Another style was tried by William Blackwood, who brought out *Middlemarch* (1871–2) and *Daniel Deronda* (1876), each in eight volumes at five shillings a volume.

Until the 1870s, when the royalty system was introduced, a successful novelist generally sold all his rights in a new novel for a lump sum. For a successful novelist this sum could be several thousand pounds, and the publisher had to use every possible expedient to recover his outlay. He might publish a three-decker for the circulating libraries, a single volume edition at a cheaper price, and parts or, alternatively, a serial in a magazine.

The three-decker novel was stopped by the action of the

circulating libraries who jibbed at the high prices. The end came rather suddenly in 1897. From 1884 to 1894 the number of three-volume novels published each year had varied between 156 and 193. After that the numbers were: 52 in 1895, 25 in 1896, 4 in 1897.

One category of nineteenth-century cheap editions has attracted especial attention, the 'yellowbacks', which began to appear about the middle of the century for sale on railway bookstalls. They were cheap editions of fiction, usually costing one or two shillings, bound in the colour which has given them their name. The binding was distinctive, consisting of glazed coloured paper laid over a foundation of strawboard. On the front cover was a picture with some bearing on the subject matter of the novel in two or more colours and on the spine there was another picture or decorative titling. On the back there was an advertisement, at first of books issued by the same publisher, later of some popular household product.

There were a number of different series from different publishers. One of the most popular was the 'Parlour Library', which included new novels as well as reprints. 'Routledge's Railway Library' copied the 'Parlour Library' in most of the details of book production. The publishers of the 'Parlour Library' brought out a non-fiction series called the 'Parlour Library of Instruction' and this too was imitated by Routledge with 'Routledge's Popular Library'. The works of popular novelists were reissued in a format similar to that of yellowbacks. Chapman & Hall brought out a series of 'Shilling Ainsworths', and the novels of G. P. R. James appeared in the 'Parlour Library'.

The great yellowback period was in the 1850s, but thereafter there was a decline in the standard of workmanship resulting from mass production. The early yellowbacks showed much variety in the design of covers, but from about 1870 this gave way to greater uniformity. There were conventional designs on the spine and cover, and spaces were left for the insertion of the name of the author and title. At first each volume was newly set up, but later worn types were used that had already been used for cloth-bound editions.

The establishment of the Detective Police Force in 1845 produced a crop of yellowbacks which were the precursors of modern detective fiction. Another group was of scandalous interest, life stories, real and imaginary, of notorious men and women.

The term 'detective story' is used loosely to describe many books in which there is virtually no detection. The genre has become popular and all sorts of other stories dealing with crime, mystery, or spying have hurried under its shade. The distinction is important for the collector, since the field is so vast that some subdivision is essential to make it manageable. One possible and easy kind of subdivision, of course, is by author. Pen-names are frequently used, thus adding to the difficulties of the collector.

Collectors have never been persuaded to take serial publications of novels seriously, even when they contain important variants and when they precede the first editions in volume form. Nineteenth-century periodicals which contain the first editions of many English classics include *The Cornhill Magazine* and Dickens's periodicals *Household Words* and *All the Year Round*. Complete sets of the serial publication of *Trilby* (1894, previously serialized in *Harper's Magazine*) and *Tess of the D'Urbervilles* (1891, previously serialized in *The Graphic* and partly also in *The Fortnightly* and *The National Observer*) can be bought for very much less than the cost of the first edition. This is because runs of periodicals take up a lot of room, are often unattractive in appearance in a mixture of binding styles, and appear to be incomplete even if they contain all the instalments of the work that gives them their interest. There is a chance here for collectors to buy sets of periodicals containing serial publications of important literary works. They are usually cheap, when they can be bought at all; they are unlikely to be reprinted; and they are liable to be destroyed because of the room they take up.

The arguments against including periodicals in a collection are mainly arguments of convenience, not of principle.

Certainly booksellers are right in saying that parts of periodicals are awkward and fragile; they soon become tattered and, at present prices, they are not worth the trouble of handling. The crux of the matter is the price. So long as they remain unpopular with collectors, they will be regarded as a nuisance by booksellers, who will encourage collectors to continue to disregard them. If collectors refuse to take that advice, the other objections to the collecting of periodicals can be overcome. For example, solander cases can be made to house single parts of periodicals.

Until about two hundred years ago there was no separate category of children's books, but many cheap books intended for adults were equally suitable for children. There were also many editions of old favourites like *Guy of Warwick* and *Bevis of Hampton* and *The Seven Champions of Christendom*. By the end of the seventeenth century religious controversy had become less fierce and there was an increase in the number of novels, often published as chapbooks at prices from a penny to sixpence. During the Commonwealth and Restoration periods chapbooks were generally quartos measuring about four inches by two and a half. It is very rare to find a popular book of the eighteenth century or earlier in even moderately good condition. In the eighteenth century chapbooks became cheaper and shorter: 16 or 32 pages in stiff paper covers. The paper cover would have a block or a mass of printer's ornaments printed on it. By about 1760 many had no cover at all and more often were not even stitched. From about 1700 small woodcuts were usual. The same blocks were borrowed and used in books by many different publishers. 'Penny Merriments' were on sale as well as religious tracts, but the tracts had a better chance of survival. Chapbooks appealed to readers of the kind who today read 'strip' cartoons in daily papers. There are occasional survivals in periodicals like *Billy's Weekly Liar*. The date on one issue in the 1920s is given as 'Octember the Twoth', which suggests that such periodicals were produced for occasional sale by street-traders or at markets rather than for regular subscribers. The date also gives an indication of the kind of humour which appealed to the readers of these ephemeral productions.

In the eighteenth century there was a tendency for printers to regard an illustrated book for children as a device for using up any old blocks and types that they happened to have in stock. It is nice to be able to record that one printer, who had made a mix-up of the blocks and printer's ornaments as well as the order of the pages, thought it proper to take full responsibility by inserting a note in Lady Fenn's *Cobwebs to Catch Flies: or, Dialogues in Short Sentences* (1783):

> The Printer thinks it but respectful to the Author, to acquaint Ladies and others, that his inattention occasioned the derangement of the Dialogues.

Most of the early children's books are heavily didactic. In the absence of anything better, they were no doubt read by children, but they were chosen by adults and the theme of virtue rewarded is nearly always prominent. Such stories continued to be written long after more readable books had become available. They were the stories against which Saki's 'Story-Teller' reacted[1] when he told the story of the little girl who had several medals for being 'horribly good'. The clinking of the medals attracted the attention of a wolf, which devoured her to the last morsel. The comments of the listeners and the narrator are interesting:

> 'It is the most beautiful story that I ever heard,' said the bigger of the small girls, with immense decision.
> 'It is the *only* beautiful story I have ever heard,' said Cyril.
> A dissentient opinion came from the aunt.
> 'A most improper story to tell to young children!'[. . .]
> 'Unhappy woman!' he observed to himself [. . .]; 'for the next six months or so those children will assail her in public with demands for an improper story!'

[1] In *Beasts and Super-Beasts*, (1914).

47

In the nineteenth century two new trends could be discerned in books for children. The first was the quenching of a thirst for information, often conveyed in the form of a catechism on such subjects as Roman history. The other trend acknowledged the beginning of an appreciation of levity and nonsense which comes to its full flower in the works of Lewis Carroll and Edward Lear. We find this trend as early as 1839, when Catherine Sinclair in *Holiday Houses* invented a giant Snap-'em-up, who was so tall that he had to climb a ladder to comb his own hair.

Illustrated books can be studied and collected from the artistic point of view or from that of the printer, who is concerned with the different processes of reproduction. The subject matter of illustrations is full of interest, and the collector can specialize in such fields as the manners of past times, costumes, portraits of famous people and pictures of buildings that no longer exist.

Illustrations are older than the invention of printing. Medieval manuscripts have illustrations, many of them magnificent, but these are not for the ordinary collector, unless he is content to limit his collection to facsimiles. This is a perfectly reasonable limitation, and some facsimiles, like those published by the Roxburghe Club or the facsimile of the Ellesmere Chaucer published by the Manchester University Press in 1913, are magnificent volumes well worth the attention of the collector. The collector of limited means must also forgo the early block-books with crude drawings carved on wood and stamped, in a brownish ink, on one side of the paper. Their subjects were simple Bible stories and episodes from the lives of the saints with pictures that were often coloured by hand.

Printing brought about a decline in the quality of illustrated books, because the illuminations of medieval manuscripts, executed with great care and patience, were replaced by crude woodcut designs which could be reproduced simultaneously with the type. A single printed sheet could be used to describe

an important event, real or fictitious, and this might be illustrated by a crude reproduction, not necessarily very appropriate, from the publisher's stock of wood-blocks. Blocks
were sold and exchanged and used again and again until they
wore out. The same illustration might be used to represent
two different towns and the same portrait block to represent
several different people.

Those who are interested in the black-and-white illustrations of the nineteenth century have expressed surprise that
they have attracted so few collectors. The reason is probably
that they are at present so cheap and plentiful. A collection of
such illustrations can easily exceed a quarter of a million
specimens. In 1842 Herbert Ingram produced the first number
of the *Illustrated London News*, which gave the news of the
week with reproductions of drawings made specially for the
purpose. An engraving would take a skilled craftsman several
days, so topical illustration was not easy. A block was divided
into square or rectangular parts and distributed among several
craftsmen. A supervising engraver corrected inconsistencies
and faults in joining.

Between 1880 and 1890 there were developments in mechanical reproduction which made illustration quicker and
cheaper. These inventions enormously increased the number
of illustrations in books and magazines. *Punch*, founded in
1841, is a great storehouse of reproductions of drawings. The
art of collecting nineteenth-century illustrations is not the
usual one of seeking for completeness in a limited part of the
field but of choosing the really good drawings from a vast
mass of mediocre work. Phil May (1864–1903) was a great
artist who rebelled against the class-consciousness of the other
Punch artists and he did much to simplify the elaborate
captions. In more recent times this process has been carried
further and much of the enjoyment to be derived from drawings in *The New Yorker* arises from the reader's reconstruction
from a single-line caption of what has gone before.

Illustrations make a strong appeal to those who dip into a
book without concentration, but to examine a number of

illustrations in detail is more tiring than reading. Illustrated books have two categories of reader: those who read the text with scarcely a glance at the illustrations, and those, chiefly the devotees of periodicals like *Punch* and *The New Yorker*, who look at the pictures and read the captions, if they are short enough, paying little attention to the text. It was one of the latter class, waiting for *Punch* in a public library, who said in an outraged voice to the reader who was not turning over the pages quickly enough: 'Do you mean to say you are *reading* it?'

If the author is himself the illustrator, his book has an added interest because of the interplay of text and illustrations. The early works of Thackeray have this kind of interest, and a book like *The Rose and the Ring* loses enormously if the illustrations are missing. Thurber enthusiasts would often find it hard to say whether their idea of the world of James Thurber is derived from the text or the drawings, and those who believe, with George Bernard Shaw, that G. K. Chesterton and Hilaire Belloc were really one very prolific author called Chesterbelloc find support for their view from the first editions of the novels of Belloc with illustrations by Chesterton, with complete harmony between text and illustrations.

To the general public, coloured illustrations have a stronger appeal than those in black and white, but their quality is often inferior. The publisher relies on the glamour of colour to distract the reader from the faults of reproduction. Just how unreliable coloured reproduction can be may be realized by putting side by side a number of coloured reproductions of a famous picture. There are often wide diversities of colour and they can't all be right.

Books with coloured illustrations are often expensive and they are very fashionable among collectors today. The original cost in England of Audubon's *Birds of America* was £174, and a copy was sold at Sotheby's in 1922 for £600; the same copy was sold in the same rooms in 1969 for £90,000, at that time the record price for a printed book. A copy was sold at Christie's in New York in 1977 for $396,000.

It is generally assumed that to build up an important collection of books is an expensive business, but this is not true. Everything depends on the choice of subject. In some fields, such as medieval manuscripts or Elizabethan quartos, a long purse is essential, but there are fields where a collection useful to both the collector and others can be built up at very little cost.

There were several cheap series in circulation during the Victorian period which, when they can be found at all, can be bought very cheaply. I have bought for a penny a volume several volumes of the series 'Chambers's Papers for the People', every volume containing half a dozen articles in small print, each of which filled 32 pages, packed with information. Less austere was the series 'Chambers's Miscellany of Useful and Entertaining Tracts', in which the print was larger and the articles more varied in length.

One of the best-known series was the Tauchnitz series of paperbacks, published on the Continent with a restriction on their import into the United Kingdom, which seems not to have been very effective, judging from the number of copies that can be found in second-hand bookshops.

Many of the series of reprints of the classics published in the second half of the nineteenth century can still be bought second-hand at prices not very different from those at which they were published, and in view of the falling value of money this means that they can be bought at a substantial reduction. They are not valuable enough to be catalogued and have to be sought in that part of the shop to which the book-hunter naturally gravitates: the modern equivalent of the fourpenny shelf. Frederick Warne published the 'Chandos Classics', which included 154 titles and sold more than five million copies. Henry Morley (1822–94), Professor of English Literature at University College, London, was indefatigable in editing cheap series, of which the best known were 'Morley's Universal Library', published by Routledge, and 'Cassell's National Library', which were published weekly at sixpence a volume in cloth, and threepence in paper covers. One of the first books that I possessed was called *The Little Folks' Out and About Book* by Chatty Cheerful, which I now believe to have been a pseudonym. The contents were mediocre but, since it was published by Cassell, there were bound in at the end advertisements of other books published by them including a list of 'Cassell's National Library'. I remember the excitement that I felt at the discovery of the treasures that were available at prices that I could afford. The series included well-known classics like the plays of Shakespeare, but the most worthwhile volumes for the collector are the minor classics which are liable to be out of print in any edition. The series includes such books as Latimer's *Sermons on the Card*, Horace Walpole's *The Castle of Otranto* and Henry Mackenzie's *The Man of Feeling*, with an index of tears, a comment on its sentimentality which shows that the editor did not take his task too seriously. The cheapest of these series was W. T. Stead's 'Penny Poets', paper-covered selections from the works of well-known poets.

Thomas Nelson and Sons have published many attractive series which can still be found on bookstalls. There are series of classics in English, French and Spanish and a 'Library of General Literature', which appeared in two formats. The earlier and more common volumes are bound in blue; the later volumes are rather taller and bound in red. The subjects range widely but the series is especially strong in essays, books of travel and memoirs. They are not for the most part great classics, but they include many books that can still be read with pleasure but which are not likely ever to be reprinted. A characteristic of the Nelson reprints is that they are printed in large type and are pleasant to read. This characteristic is not shared by every series of cheap reprints. A particularly bad offender is Dick's series of 'Standard Plays', a long series containing two plays in a volume printed in minute type and sold for a penny.

Probably the best-known of the series of reprints of the classics is 'Everyman's Library', begun by J. M. Dent in 1906 when he was 57. It had been preceded by 'The Camelot

Classics', published by a firm with the misleading name of Walter Scott Ltd., and the 'Illustrated Pocket Classics', published by Collins. The success of 'Everyman's Library' nearly ruined the publisher, since the sales were so much greater than he expected that he was short of capital to cover the period between the payment of his printer's bills and the receipt of payments from booksellers. The general editor was Ernest Rhys, a former mining engineer, who had been chosen to edit 'The Camelot Classics' because the publishers confused him with Professor (afterwards Sir) John Rhys, the eminent Celtic scholar,[1] He had no problems in selecting the first two hundred volumes or so. The books in the series are numbered, and the first two hundred titles form a good selection for those who like to have their list of the world's best books chosen for them. Some of the later titles cause surprise to a reader of today in that they do not seem to have an importance proportionate to their length. Grote's *History of Greece* in twelve volumes and J. A. Froude's histories of the English Tudors are little read today and many of these volumes have been allowed to go out of print, but the series as a whole provides good scope for a collector with plenty of shelf-room but limited means. If the full series of more than a thousand volumes seems too ambitious an aim, the collector can confine his attention to one of the dozen or so subsections, such as Fiction or Biography, into which the series is divided.

When a series has been in existence for many years it is often redesigned to make it conform to changes of taste, and a comparison of early and late volumes provides an interesting comment on these changes. The earlier volumes in 'Everyman's Library' had gilt decoration on the spines, end-papers with flowing patterns and crowded title-pages with floral decoration showing the influence of the Kelmscott Press. After the First World War the design of the whole book was simplified and later the size of each volume was slightly enlarged, producing books whose description as pocket edi-

[1] See Ernest Rhys, *Everyman Remembers* (Dent, 1931), pp. 75 f.

tions would make a tailor wince. The latest stage reflects the growing popularity of paperbacks by making selected titles available in that form. Similar changes have taken place in the 'World's Classics', taken over by the Oxford University Press from Grant Richards. Some of the early volumes were printed on thick paper, which makes them dumpy, and with small type that is avoided in the later editions.

Another kind of book that can be bought cheaply, because booksellers grudge the room that it takes up, is the set of volumes made up of periodical parts. Such sets were published in large numbers during the nineteenth and twentieth centuries and have made fortunes for their publishers and editors, who rightly assumed that unsophisticated readers would buy weekly or fortnightly parts and have them bound by the publishers without realizing how expensive the complete set would be. Readers were willing to wait a long time for the completion of a set: *Chambers's Encyclopaedia* was published in 520 weekly parts between 1859 and 1868. Histories of wars were a popular subject. Alfred Harmsworth did much to develop this type of publication with the assistance of his two editors J. A. Hammerton and Arthur Mee. One of their less successful ventures was *The World's Great Books in Outline*, of which two editions were published. It catered for readers who wanted to know more about the classics of world literature without going to the length of reading them. The publication of the first edition gave rise to a squib recording a supposed conversation between the two editors:

> 'This Gibbon in ten pages
> Must be cut down to three.'
> 'It can't be done,' said Hammerton.
> 'It must be done,' said Mee.

Probably the best-known and best-loved of these periodical publications was Arthur Mee's *Children's Encyclopaedia*, which appeared in several editions during the first half of the twentieth century.

The present century has seen the 'paperback revolution', and there is an obvious difference between the appearance of the shelves of an older and a younger book-buyer. The older generation have shelves filled with sober – some would say dingy – cloth-bound books, usually without dust-jackets. Dust-jackets have now become more attractive, with the result that book-buyers do not want to throw them away, and there has been a great increase in the number of 'quality paperbacks' in stiff glossy covers. There has also been a change in distribution. Houses in which at one time it would have been hard to find a single book are now likely to have a shelf full of paperback modern novels, which show signs of having been well read. The change is largely due to the activities of the publishers of Penguin Books, which first appeared in 1935.

In attributing the paperback revolution to Penguin Books two qualifications are necessary. First, I am speaking primarily of Great Britain. Paperback editions had long been normal on the Continent as they had in England, before the introduction of cheap cloth bindings in the early nineteenth century replaced them and relieved the book-collector of the necessity of employing his own binder. The second qualification is that even in Great Britain Penguin Books were not the first series of cheap paperback reprints. More than fifty years before them George Hutchinson had published a series of sixpenny reprints, and in the 1920s Ernest Benn had published a long series of non-fiction books entitled 'Benn's Sixpenny Library' and a series of 'Sixpenny Poets'. The managing director responsible for them was Victor Gollancz, who started his own imprint as a publisher in 1928. The 'Sixpenny Library', with orange-coloured covers, was an especially worthwhile enterprise with contributions by world-famous scholars. The books are not often seen nowadays, no doubt because their slim, unpretentious appearance and the inclusion of the word 'sixpenny' in the title of the series made booksellers unwilling to stock them or to charge the price that they are worth. They are the sort of book that the impecunious book-buyer can very profitably look out for.

What was new about Penguin Books was the energy and enterprise shown in developing new ventures and in dis-covering new sales outlets which had not previously been taken seriously by publishers. The familiar orange-coloured Penguins were quickly followed by non-fiction Pelicans, Penguin Specials dealing with current affairs, crime novels, and a series of Puffin Books for children. The Second World War encouraged a popular interest in current affairs and pro-vided a large public of new readers with time on their hands. Firewatchers welcomed cheap and expendable books, and dislike of the black-out kept many people at home. New titles appeared with commendable frequency. The series gave a new lease of life to many best-sellers of an earlier generation. From the point of view of the collector Penguins have the attraction of cheapness and, since they were liable to go out of print at short notice, they appeal to the love of the chase in every collector. There is not much fun in collecting a series which can be bought complete over the counter from a book-seller. The chief disadvantage is that they were printed on cheap paper, which was not intended to last, and the earlier volumes are already brown round the edges. This complaint cannot be brought against the picture books, the King Penguins, which closely resemble the German Insel Bücher, and they have already become collectors' items.

CHAPTER III

THE MAKING OF BOOKS

BOOK-COLLECTING is more than acquisition, and it is
a knowledge of bibliography that makes the difference between the accumulator and the collector.
Bibliography is the study of books as physical objects; it bears
the same relation to collecting as reading bears to book-
buying. The bibliographer and the collector do not always
have the same interests. Condition is important to the collector but not to the bibliographer, and to a bibliographer the
chief importance of rarity is that it makes it harder for him to
assemble the raw materials of his craft.

The first step in linking collecting with bibliography is to
learn how to describe each book systematically with a view
to comparing it with other copies that may be found in
catalogues or bibliographies. The amount of detail in the
description will vary from book to book and from collector
to collector, but the description of a book which the collector
takes seriously may become very elaborate. It begins with a
transcription of the title-page, indicating the kind of type
used with a vertical stroke to mark the end of each line.
Then comes a collation of the contents to indicate how many
gatherings and what signatures are used. Such a collation is
the best way of making sure that the book is complete and
of recording mistakes in the pagination, which are frequent
in early books. Next, illustrations have to be listed with
indications where they occur in the book and whether they
form part of the collation or whether they are pasted in or
wrapped round gatherings of text. Are the end-papers blank
or do they contain advertisements? Are they coloured or
decorated? Next the bibliographer has to note the colour

and texture of paper used for the text, illustrations and end-papers. Is the paper laid or wove? Are the edges of the pages trimmed, coloured or gilt? Often the top edges are different from the rest. What material is used for binding and what colour is it? If cloth, the texture should be noted. If it is grained, does the grain run horizontally or vertically? The lettering on the sides and the spine should be transcribed. It often differs from the title as given on the title-page. After this the bibliographer may turn his attention to variations and issue-problems.

Some booksellers have been outstandingly good bibliographers but others have tended to resent the time that detailed examination takes up and the fact that, when knowledge of the subject becomes widespread, it makes the 'wrong' books difficult to sell. The time taken in the study of bibliography is part of the bookseller's justification for a high margin of profit. Unfortunately, the bookseller who knows nothing of bibliography often expects the same margin as the expert bookseller.

Bibliography may be a nuisance to a bookseller, but it is available to his customers as well as himself so he must accept it, just as an art dealer has to accept the knowledge of an art expert and, if possible, become one himself. The 'wrong' book may become unsaleable but the one proved to be 'right' becomes more valuable.

Popular fallacies about old books are often the result of faulty observation. Most book-collectors have been approached by someone saying, 'I have an old book that has *f*'s for *s*'s. Is it valuable?' The answer is likely to be 'No', but what is here described as an 'f' is usually a long 's', which differs from an 'f' in that the short horizontal stroke half way up the letter is only on the left-hand side instead of cutting across the vertical stroke, as in an 'f'.

The technical language of bibliography is for the most part made up of the terms of several different trades: the paper-maker (for example laid paper), the type-founder (Caslon Old Face, 12-point, pica), the printer (signatures) and the binder (blind tooling). All collectors need to know some terms from the vocabulary of book manufacture (gothic, italic, roman), book distribution (publication, remainder), and condition (foxing, worming, association copy, presentation copy). It is well to know the most common kinds of misprint, misgathering and faulty blocking or binding. Misprints can be found because letters are set in the wrong order or words misdivided, or because the type is not locked securely enough in the chase so that, after a few sheets have been run off, one or more letters fall out and may be wrongly replaced. Changes may be made by last-minute corrections from the author after printing has begun, or because the book is not ready within the year specified on the back of the title-page.

Half-titles, when they exist, are necessary to completeness though books were issued without them. In some books copies with a half-title are so scarce as to suggest that part of the edition was issued without it. When blank leaves are part of a gathering it is reasonable to demand them if a copy is to be regarded as complete, but in very old or rare books their absence may be tolerated.

Some technical terms are used with varying meanings and these have led to some confusion in terminology. For example, *edition*, *impression*, *issue* and *state* have all been the subject of argument.

One of the reasons for a careful description is that it enables the bibliographer to decide whether the book in question is a first edition. It is generally known that this is a matter to which collectors attach importance, but it is not generally realized why they do so. There are ignoble reasons, such as fashion or habit, but there are also sensible ones. One path to the study of first editions is by way of textual criticism. This is less formidable than it sounds. Textual criticism is not the preserve of the scholar. Newspapers are so carelessly printed nowadays that a reader often has to resort to textual criticism in order to make sense of them. He has to do the same in reading a novel published within the last century or so. A publisher bringing out a new edition of a text written in the seventeenth century will take it for granted that he must employ an editor to establish the text, but if he is publishing a reprint of a Victorian novel the chances are that he will just hope for the best and produce an edition that is a copy of a copy with an accumulation of errors of transcription. There are honourable exceptions, such as the Clarendon Press editions of some of the novels of Dickens, but these are expensive and are heavily outnumbered by careless reprints. If such a reprint falls into the hands of a careful reader, there are likely to be passages which cause him to say 'Did the author really say that?' The best way of finding out, though it does not provide a complete answer, is to consult the first edition.

It is well known that first editions are valuable because they are most likely to present the original thoughts of the author. It is less generally remembered that the last edition published in the lifetime of the author has a special value, because it may contain the author's final revisions, though it may not have been revised under his direction.

Of most books the first is the only edition. One author was heard to admit: 'It's second editions of my books that are rare.' Of illustrated and finely-printed books the first editions will be the clearest because they are printed before the plates and type have become worn. Evidence that a book is a first edition is largely negative; it is a good rough and ready rule that a book is likely to be a first edition if there is no evidence that it is not.

There is often confusion between an edition and an impression. An edition is any number of copies of a book printed from one setting of type, while an impression is a number of copies printed at one time, and an edition may consist of a number of impressions. The distinction arises because the type need not be dispersed immediately after an impression has been printed. In earlier days it was more difficult to keep type standing than it is today and labour was cheap; therefore each new printing was often from a new setting of type. Even today there is some expense involved in keeping type standing, and a new edition may involve revision by the author.

If the differences between two copies are such that one cannot be shown to be later than the other, they are said to be different *states* of that edition. A mark of identification that distinguishes one issue of an edition from another is known as a *point*. It may be such a detail as a misprint or a broken letter, an ornament upside down, a different colour or texture of binding, an alteration by the author, a different quality of paper, changes in the tint of the top edges, the colour of the end-papers or the lettering on the cover.

We have a good deal of evidence for deciding the priority of two editions with the same date on the back of the title-page. We have the publisher's records, the date of the acquisition of the book by the British Museum or Library of Congress, watermarks, the date of the advertisements, if any, letters and diaries of the author, and misprints in the text. When a collector buys both copies of a disputed first edition, he is not just taking the easy way out of a difficult problem; he is providing the material to enable a bibliographer to study the question.

The argument about Anglo-American first editions is comparatively recent. The older view was that the first British edition of a book by a British author was the first edition. The discovery by bibliographers that an American edition sometimes antedated the British edition was resisted by collectors and booksellers who saw the prices of their possessions fall.

We have also to distinguish between priority of issue and priority of publication. An author may die or a publisher go out of business or there may be a legal ban on publication after a book has been set up and bound but before a single copy has been sold or given away. The description 'First published edition' is generally an indication that there may be an earlier privately printed or suppressed edition.

Limiting the size of an edition is a perfectly valid way of

increasing its appeal to collectors and so making it possible to produce attractive editions that might not otherwise repay the cost of production. With such editions experiments in book production are possible and a better quality of paper can be used. Abuses creep in when an edition is 'limited' to an excessively large number of copies. If the number of copies to which an edition is limited is larger than the number that the publisher might reasonably expect to sell, the limitation has little meaning, and we sometimes find the ultimate absurdity, a limited edition that has been remaindered.

Printers have established certain conventions in the setting up of books which readers have learnt to accept without realizing that they exist, but a departure from these conventions would startle many readers. For example, most printers try to avoid ending a chapter with a page of only two or three lines or allowing a page to begin with the half-line at the end of a paragraph. To avoid such an unusual position, it may be necessary to save or lose a line by adjusting the spaces between words. Such adjustment is a normal practice to secure a straight right-hand margin, though recently some books have been printed without such a straight margin. Another convention is to begin a new chapter at the top of a new page, leaving a space blank at the foot of the last page of the preceding chapter. Books printed in wartime often had to forgo this elegance.

We have become accustomed to certain proportions in the margins on a page. The top margin is nearly always narrower than the lower margin because the optical centre of the type-area is higher than the actual centre. The inner margin is approximately half the outer margin. The reason is that the unit is not a single page but the two facing pages seen together when the book is opened.

As every book-buyer knows, printing costs have increased enormously in the last few years. The chief hope for the future lies in the possibility of replacing mechanical typesetting by photographic composing machines. The advantages are obvious: the saving of labour, weight and storage space and the saving of money at present tied up in standing type. One disadvantage is that photographic methods will not give a really black image, and the printed type tends to look grey.

Extreme variations in the size of books is one of the aberrations of book production. One can appreciate the jest of an edition of *Gulliver's Travels* in which the 'Voyage to Lilliput' was a minute volume and the 'Voyage to Brobdignag' was of giant size, though anyone who bought a copy would have storage problems. The Vernon Manuscript, a well-known anthology of Middle English poetry in the Bodleian, has a page whose written area alone is seventeen and a half by twelve and a half inches,[1] and towards the end of the nineteenth century it was a common practice to publish large paper editions of standard-sized books at a higher price for collectors. The greater size was achieved by simply increasing the width of the margins, and the result was generally unattractive because the balance between text and page-size found in a well-planned book was destroyed. Conversely, pocket editions printed from the plates of the first edition of a book often have margins that are too narrow. There have at times been crazes for the production of very small books, and some collectors specialize in them. Collectors of small books make a distinction between books printed from type and those printed from engraved plates or produced by a photographic process. They tend to regard photography as cheating.

In our enjoyment of reading we are all influenced to some extent by the materials of which a book is made, and one material that we cannot avoid is the paper on which it is printed. A few copies of early printed books were often printed on vellum. The chief motive was to produce a costly and sumptuous volume, no doubt usually for presentation,

---

[1] W. D. Macray, *Annals of the Bodleian Library* (OUP, 1890), p. 144.

but another motive was to produce a book that would stand up to the wear and tear that schoolbooks and theological treatises had to endure.

Before the discovery of new materials in the nineteenth century, paper was expensive, and printers hoarded it over long periods. This hoarding explains one feature of some early printed books: the use of two or three kinds of paper in one book. Linen and cotton rags were ideal for paper-making since their fibres were long, elastic and durable, but, with the introduction of power-presses in the early nine-teenth century, editions became larger and other materials had to be found. Esparto grass is now used for most better-class paper. For newspapers and cheap editions of novels wood pulp is used, although the fibres are short and brittle. The paper soon turns yellow and begins to crumble at the edges. If paper is found to be made from wood pulp or esparto grass it cannot be earlier than the nineteenth century. Inexperienced book-buyers tend to think that a thick book must be better than a thin one. Consequently cheap books are often printed on loosely compacted paper consisting largely of air. Such paper soils easily and does not wear well. It is unfortunate that the two categories that are most likely to be printed on this bulky paper are those which are likely to have to stand up to rough usage: children's books and novels.

Art paper is given a special coating of glazed china clay to present a smooth surface on which to print half-tone blocks. Its disadvantage is that the coating weakens the paper and makes it so brittle that a fold quickly becomes a crack, and that is one of the reasons why plates fall out of books. Art paper is very heavy and if a whole book is printed on such paper, it is awkward to handle and expensive to send through the post.

Most papers receive some kind of polishing, known as calendering, by being passed between rollers at great pres-sure. John Baskerville, the eighteenth-century Birmingham printer, pressed pages between hot metal plates, giving them

an exceptional finish. Laid paper shows the pattern made by
the paper-maker's tray. The wide-apart thick lines are called
chain-lines and the close thin lines at right angles to these are
called *wire-lines*.

Some books are printed on coloured papers and Sterne
imposed various eccentricities on the printer of *Tristram
Shandy*; whole pages were blacked out and one page was
marbled.

A watermark is the figure or device often seen on a sheet
of paper when held up to the light. It is the result of sewing
to the mould used in paper-making an ornamental figure in
wire or thin brass, which leaves an impression on the paper
by making it thinner and more translucent. Watermarks are
important because they may indicate the approximate date
when the paper was made and they are often overlooked by
forgers. Since watermarks are difficult to imitate, forgers
have generally tried to obtain genuine old paper. W. H.
Ireland, the forger, said in his *Confessions* that his great difficulty was to obtain the paper. He selected half-sheets from
account books of the reign of Charles I and chose half-
sheets without watermarks. A bookseller allowed him, for
five shillings, to take the fly-leaves from all the folios and
quartos in his shop.

End-papers are the leaves inserted by the binder between
the covers and the leaves of a book. They are often of different paper from the body of the book, although, as a result of
wartime economies, they may sometimes be of the same
paper and form part of the signatures and pagination. They
are the province of the binder, not the printer. They generally consist of two conjugate leaves, one pasted to the cover,
the other free. The former is called a *paste-down*, the latter is
often called a *fly-leaf*, but the latter term is best kept to denote
a blank leaf that appears at the beginning of the first gathering or at the end of the last gathering of a book; it is part of
the raw materials of the printer, not of the binder. The lack
of such a leaf may drastically reduce the price of a second-
hand book. When the leaf is not completely blank, there is

some confusion in terminology between *fly-title* and *half-title*. Some bibliographers use *half-title* for a leaf that gives the name of the book but not that of the author or publisher, and it normally immediately precedes the title-page, while they use *fly-title* for leaves that introduce new sections or divisions within the book. A *sub-title* is a literary rather than a bibliographical term. It describes an amplification of the name of the book or an alternative to it, as in *Vanity Fair, A Novel Without a Hero* or *Eric, or Little by Little*. Alternative titles are less common now than they were in the nineteenth century.

In the earliest printed books there are none of the 'prelims' with which we are familiar today: title-pages, half-titles, tables of contents, prefaces, dedications, and so forth. The title was part of the text of the book itself and consisted of the opening words of the book, generally preceded by the word *Incipit* 'Here begins'. The name of the printer was given at the end of the book in a *colophon*, but the name of the author was generally not given, on the assumption that it was either well-known or unimportant.

When title-pages were introduced they were wordy, and quite unimportant words were in large type. Two copies of a book may have slightly different title-pages because the title was often set up twice on two halves of the same sheet of paper. An old title-page might be used unchanged for a new edition. Some books had two title-pages, the first engraved with elaborate decorations and the second printed.

The early printers each had a stock of ornaments, rules and decorative initials, which were highly prized and passed down from father to son. It is often possible to deduce the approximate date of a book from the extent to which these ornaments show signs of wear.

From the late seventeenth century onwards advertisements were included in many books as an integral part of the volume. The practice of inserting leaves of advertisements as separate gatherings, often on different paper, became common in the nineteenth and early twentieth centuries. These advertisements provide evidence of publication date. There are some *ghost-titles*, books that were advertised but never published. Advertisements which form an integral part of the book are not likely to be removed. Self-contained gatherings of advertisements are sometimes removed or may never have been there; if a stock of inserted catalogues ran out, a binder might produce copies of the same book, some with and some without advertisements. If the advertisements are several years later than the date on the title-page, the book is likely to be a late issue.

A practice that adds to the interest of eighteenth-century books, though it is less common today, is the use of cancels when an author fears that he has written something libellous or seditious. A *cancel* has been defined by R. W. Chapman as 'a leaf or leaves (sometimes part of a leaf) intended to be substituted for the corresponding part of a book as originally printed'.[1] If any copies survive without the changes, we have two issues of the same edition. The printer has the choice of replacing the whole sheet or a single leaf, which has to be pasted on to the stub of the leaf that has been removed. The presence of a stub does not prove that a cancel has been made, but it is a warning to be checked by comparison with other copies. To avoid ambiguity Dr Chapman coined the expression *folium cancellandum* to denote the leaf to be excised and *folium cancellans* to denote the leaf that replaces it.

The reason why cancels were more common in the eighteenth century than they are today is that editions were smaller and therefore less work was involved in making them. Philip Gaskell has pointed out that there are usually over sixty cancels in the 1773 Baskerville edition of Ariosto's *Orlando Furioso*.[2] They have grown more expensive to produce, and therefore more rare, as a result of the use of modern machinery, whereas in the eighteenth century they

[1] *Cancels* (Constable, 1930), p. 5.
[2] *The Rothschild Library Catalogue* (CUP, 1954), p. 713.

were sometimes used merely to correct minor errors of punctuation or syntax.

There is an allusion to the use of cancels in Boswell's *Life of Johnson*.[1] Oliver Goldsmith in his *Animated Nature* (1774) told the story of a mathematician who yawned so violently in one of his own lectures that he dislocated his jaw. The mathematician's son claimed that the story was untrue but found that he had no legal redress. The bookseller, on being approached, 'agreed very handsomely to have the leaf on which it was contained cancelled, and reprinted without it, at his own expense'.

A cancelling leaf is often given a distinctive signature to show where it is to be inserted; such signatures are to be found on both single leaves and gatherings. An indication of the presence of a cancel is often given by the paper, especially if it is laid. Do the chain-lines run the same way as the rest of the book and are they the same distance apart? The water-mark may also give a clue. The running title on a cancel is likely to be out of alignment with the rest of the book or it may be set with different spacing.

Like dust-wrappers and book-plates, bindings began by serving a strictly practical purpose, but the craftsmen who made them were not content with utility, and bindings have developed as independent works of art that have an interest quite apart from the contents of the book. The early printers were often their own binders. Binding is not an integral part of the book, which is complete without it. At one time the book was so published, to be bound after the sale in a style to suit the taste of the purchaser. Some early Middle Eastern bindings consist of a kind of wallet or casing of soft-tooled leather lightly attached to the back of the book. The earliest bindings in Western Europe are of wood, using heavy boards to keep the vellum flat. They are sometimes inlaid with precious stones or covered with carvings. Sometimes ivory

[1] Ed. Birkbeck Hill (OUP, 1934), vol. III, p. 15.

or metal was used instead of wood. Leather or pigskin might be folded over the wooden boards. To make the binding less heavy, the wooden boards were replaced by millboard, made of cuttings of hemp or jute, or pasteboard, made by pasting several sheets of paper together. Printer's waste from earlier books was used to make the pasteboard or as end-papers, and to this practice we owe our knowledge of fragments of many books not otherwise known.

The earliest printed books were not ranged on shelves with their spines facing outwards, as they are today. They were laid flat on reading-desks or shelves, and therefore great size was not much of a nuisance. Titles were written on labels attached to the front cover, sometimes protected by transparent horn. Books printed on vellum were liable to swell open through damp or heat, and to avert this swelling, catches and clamps were fixed to the fore-edges of the binding to keep the book closed. In chained libraries, books stood upright on the shelves with the fore-edges outward, with the chain fastened to the foot of the front board. Imperfect copies of older books came into existence because the binders' workmen would bind up extra copies from old sheets and sell them to booksellers or the public at reduced prices. Anthologies were especially liable to be treated in this way.

William Edwards of Halifax (1723–1808) and his two sons developed a new method of decorating vellum for book-binding. After the loose, spongy part of the skin had been scraped, the part to be ornamented was soaked in pearl ash and subjected to pressure, making it transparent. Designs or views were then painted on the underside of the vellum and backed with white paper. Edwards is often credited with the invention of fore-edge paintings, but these were known a century before his time. Many of the examples in circulation are quite recent.

In the eighteenth century it was usual for books to be sold in temporary bindings of thin boards, covered with grey-blue paper and with a paper label stuck on the spine. From about 1820 books began to appear with their boards covered in cloth instead of paper, and by the middle of the century cloth bindings had superseded boards and labels. From 1853 cheap yellowbacks made of pasteboard bearing gaudy illustrations were used for novels. Ordinary cloth soiled easily and was unworkable and expensive and it was soon replaced by publisher's cloth, a nineteenth-century innovation.

In the early days of the three-decker, publishers issued novels in unbound sheets, and distributors bound them for sale to the libraries. In 1842 Charles Edward Mudie founded his circulating library in London and he bought novels in sheets, doing his own binding. Soon afterwards publishers adopted the present practice of issuing their novels bound.

The introduction of casing instead of binding was roughly contemporary with the adoption of publisher's cloth. In casing the gatherings are sewn to tapes and a piece of gauze is glued along the sewn spine. The case is made separately and the book is attached to the inside of the case by glueing down the overlaps of the gauze and the tapes. End-papers are then pasted to the insides of the boards.

The use of the term 'uncut' often leads to misunderstanding. It is necessary to distinguish between the terms *uncut* and *unopened*. The first indicates that the binder has avoided the use of a guillotine to trim the edges of the pages, while the second means that the purchaser of the book has not used a paper-knife on an uncut copy. This is a technical use of the term, since a book with trimmed edges might never have been opened and a reader accustomed to handling books would be able to detect the fact, but it would not as a rule be described as unopened.

Half-binding and quarter-binding are the result of attempts to gain the strength of leather binding while cutting down on the cost. Leather is used at the points of greatest wear: the spine and the corners. Half-binding was common in the nineteenth century. Whether its use is worthwhile depends a good deal on the relative cost of labour and materials at the time of binding. Today the trouble and expense incurred by half-binding outweigh the cost of binding a book entirely in the stronger of the two materials used. Half-binding is still fairly common in the production of ledgers, which are large enough to make a full leather binding expensive but which have to stand a good deal of heavy use.

A refinement that adds slightly to the cost of production is the gilding of the top edges of pages. After the pages have been trimmed, the book is squeezed in a press and the edges are washed over with a preparation of red chalk. The edges are then brushed, size is applied and gold leaf is put on immediately and afterwards burnished. Gold leaf is so thin that its use does not add very much to the cost of production, but cheaper substitutes are sometimes used. Silver is not suitable because it tarnishes easily, and the most common substitute is colour harmonizing with the book-cover. The advantages of gilding are not merely decorative; the gold is a protection against dust, and one of the minor pleasures of life for a book-collector is to wipe the gilt edges with a soft duster and to see the brilliance of the gold restored.

Yapp edges are sometimes found, where limp leather projects considerably beyond the pages with the aim of keeping their edges clean. The yapp edges are usually soft and floppy, but sometimes they are stiff and permanently turned at right angles to the board. Such bindings enjoy the widest use among readers to whom the possession of a book is something of a novelty. They are found especially on bibles and editions of *The Rubaiyat of Omar Khayyam* bound in flexible leather and sold as suitable for Christmas gifts.

Instead of being sewn, cheap books are sometimes held together by metal staples. The latest stage is that which we associate with telephone directories and some paperbacks: the gatherings are trimmed into separate leaves, which are stuck together at the inner margins by gutta percha or rubber solution.

A box made to look like a book is a useful compromise between lovers of original condition and those who like to have an attractive appearance on their shelves.

One of the most frequent complaints made by reviewers

is that the book that they are criticizing has no index. The presence of an index is an indication that a book is intended to be used in part as a work of reference, whether the user has previously read it or not. So many books are published that most bookmen get into the way of forming a provisional estimate of the importance of a book by a process that, to an unpractised observer, looks very much like sniffing at it. I once heard a bookman, when asked by an earnest lady whether he had read a particular book, reply cautiously, 'Well, I've reviewed it'. The earnest lady was shocked, as the speaker intended that she should be.

Titles of books present problems for both author and publisher. The first requirement of a title is to give some idea of what the book is about, but some authors are even more conscious of the value of a title in attracting the interest of a potential reader. Titles based on quotations are useful in giving those who recognize the quotation a fuller idea of the subject of the book than can be provided by the three or four words that the author usually allows himself. It would be possible to compile a long list of well-known novels, such as *If Winter Comes* and *For Whom the Bell Tolls* which received their titles in this way. If the source of the quotation is not well-known, the author may give a hint by quoting the title in its context among the prelims. Writers of detective stories have the same sort of problem as newspaper sports commentators. They have to describe a number of events which resemble one another so closely that it is hard to achieve variety in the language used to describe them. Thus there is a certain sameness about the titles of detective stories, to which P. G. Wodehouse called attention when he made one of his characters say that he had been reading *Death at Some Dashed Place or Other*.

Booksellers need to have ingenuity and tact to enable them to correct some of the titles that they are asked for, since oral transmission can play havoc with an unfamiliar title. Such silent corrections are not news, but a bookseller's occasional failures become news to be quoted with amusement or derision. Lord Lytton's *Ernest Maltravers* became *Earnest Small Travellers* and J. M. Barrie's *A Window in Thrums* became *Widow's Thumbs*. Hall and Knight's *Algebra* is cunningly disguised as *All the Night's Algebra* and *Reminiscences of Judge Hawkins* became *The Many Sins of Judge Hawkins*. Classification can produce howlers, such as the inclusion of Ouida's *Moths* under entomology and Rider Haggard's *King Solomon's Mines* under Old Testament history. The customer who ordered *The History of the Uninhabited Islands of the Pacific, by One of the Natives* had not thought deeply enough on the subject, and a woman who ordered a book by Bishop Wilberforce returned it because it said quite clearly on the title-page that it was by Samuel Oxon. A good deal of trouble is caused to booksellers by the newspaper practice of giving to a review a headline different from the title of the book, with the result that the customer remembers the headline rather than the title. One harassed bookseller said 'How could I be expected to know that a customer who asked for *Home Brewed and Mild* really wanted *Round the Home of a Yorkshire Parson* or that one who ordered *A Backstair Biography* wanted Mrs Crawford's *Victoria— Queen and Ruler*?'

Publishers try to avoid titles that suggest that a book has narrow or local interest. Their solution is to choose a title worded in the most general terms and to give the real subject as a sub-title.

Titles that have misled unskilled cataloguers have often been quoted; perhaps the best known is *Mill on the Floss* followed by — *On Liberty*. A less familiar example is 'Shelley's *Prometheus* (unbound)'. There are some catalogue entries where it is not certain whether a description applies to the condition of a book or its subject-matter, as in 'Sterne's *Tristram Shandy* (a little loose)'.

When titles are long and books slim the binder has a problem, since there is no room for a horizontal title and the title has to run up or down the spine. We could get used to either practice, but unfortunately there is no uniformity. One writer on book production has described the present situation:

> Bookshops began to find that rows of thin books came together, some with spines running up and some down, and the book-buyer, with his head wagging from side to side, began to look like an inverted pendulum. But nothing was done to mend matters.[1]

The strongest argument in support of the runners-down is that when a book is laid flat on a table with the face upward, lettering that runs down the spine will be easily legible whereas lettering that runs up the spine will be upside-down. Until publishers reach agreement, book-buyers have to be patient, but they have a right to protest when, as happens surprisingly often, books from the same publisher are published with some titles running up and others running down.

Dust-jackets to protect the covers of books came into use in the course of the nineteenth century and had become normal by the end of the century. At first they were of plain paper and were intended as a temporary protection to suffice until the purchasers could have the books bound. Cheaper production and larger editions led to the purchase of books by readers who had no desire for rebinding, and temporary bindings in paper or boards gave way to edition bindings intended to be permanent. Dust-jackets came to be used for advertisements either of books by the same author or publisher or, less happily, of miscellaneous products like soap or patent medicines. The front flap is generally reserved for the blurb, a summary of the contents of the book with a few words about the status of the author. Problems began to arise for collectors when publishers realized that dust-jackets could be made attractive and so act as an inducement to

[1] Sean Jennett, *The Making of Books* (Faber, 1951), pp. 437 f.

74

casual browsers to buy the book. They are now far too attractive to throw away. The problem for the collector is: can a book be regarded as complete without its dust-jacket? Dust-jackets have something in common with book-plates in that both began by serving a simple utilitarian purpose, but in course of time they have become so attractive as to be collectable in their own right. In each case the collector has to face the problem that he does not know how long they have formed part of the books with which they are now kept. Pictorial book-jackets can greatly enhance the attractiveness of a book, and some publishers pay special attention to them. The topographical books published by Batsford have jackets that most purchasers would probably like to preserve, and readers with specialized interests have found in the bright yellow jackets of Victor Gollancz a useful indication that they need seek no further. A tattered dust-jacket is an unattractive sight and a collection of dust-jackets without their books seems to lack something. Public libraries usually solve the problem by providing a transparent plastic cover for the dust-wrapper, thus providing additional protection for the book and brightening its appearance on the shelf.

Since dust-jackets will often be detached from their books, it is important that they should not contain information that is not repeated in the body of the book, and publishers should resist the temptation to insert in the book the name of the designer of the dust-jacket.

CHAPTER IV

THE CARE OF BOOKS

MARRIED book-collectors face special problems. A drawing by James Thurber shows an angry wife confronting her husband in a book-lined room with the words, 'There isn't room in this house for belles-lettres and me both.' Sometimes the plight of a book-collector's wife can arouse the sympathy of all but the most hardened of bibliophiles. Wilmarth Lewis describes a visit that he paid to Seymour de Ricci:

> His flat was on the ground floor in the rue Boissière. Only a ground floor could support the weight of his thirty thousand auction-sale catalogues. Mme de Ricci came in while I was telling her husband of my problem. We stood in the drawing-room, which had sale catalogues from floor to ceiling, on the tables, chairs, and floor. 'Books!' she cried with loathing. 'Would you like to see where I hang my dresses?' I followed her into her bedroom, where she threw open the closet door. There, leaving no space for a single dress, were rows and rows of auction-sale catalogues. 'Books everywhere!' she said with hatred and despair, and abruptly left us.[1]

Charles Sarolea of Edinburgh, who was perhaps the last of the really large-scale collectors, is said to have solved the problem by telling his wife from time to time that she ought to have a holiday. When she left home for a few days he quickly rang up the booksellers who were keeping large stocks of books for him to tell them that now was the time to deliver them. When his wife returned, she thought that

[1] *Collector's Progress* (Constable, 1952), p. 166.

THE CARE OF BOOKS

there seemed to be a lot more books than when she went away, but with such a large total number, of the order of 100,000, she couldn't be sure.

Part of a wife's problem is that of finding room for the books; another is that piles of books make it harder to keep a house clean; a third is the fear that the book-lover is spending too much money on books. One book-collector tried to meet this objection by asking his booksellers to indicate two prices. The first was the real purchase price, which he paid without question and never asked for a receipt. The second price was written inside the book with the stipulation that it must never exceed three-and-sixpence. The arrangement worked well and it continued to have good results after the book-collector's death. His widow regretted all that she had said about wasting money on books when she found what a lot of books her husband had apparently bought for three-and-sixpence which she was able to sell for several pounds.

It is generally assumed that 'book-collector' is a masculine noun, and there is no doubt that men outnumber women as collectors, but there are examples of husbands who are puzzled and indignant at finding that they have inadvertently married a book-collector. The following letter (quoted from the *News of the World* in *The Book Collector*, 1976, p. 389) is written in the simple language which has often been found to accompany deep emotion:

> My wife's hobby is collecting books. Many of her books are never read at all. She refuses to join the public library, though I've begged her to, hoping it would cure her. *R.J., Thanet, Kent.*

Even those scholars who might be expected to be tolerant of book-collectors are not always so. W. C. Hazlitt in *The Book-Collector* (1904, p. 164) says with the prim disapproval of a Victorian governess:

> Literary acquisitions are unfortunately apt to occupy space, and, save in very exceptional cases, to deteriorate in value.

How should books be arranged on the shelves: in order of subject, size, date of acquisition, or alphabetically? Classification by subject matter has the advantage that it makes the use of a catalogue unnecessary; the position of the book on its appropriate shelf places it near to books of related interest. However, it is usually necessary to make concessions to other methods of arrangement. The preservation of books in good condition is best achieved if books of similar size are kept together, because tall books support one another. Very tall books are best kept on their sides. You can often see on the back of a large book a small rectangle of a different colour from the rest of the binding, the result of keeping a small book next to a large one, by fading of the exposed surface of the larger book.

Classification by date of acquisition is in effect no classification at all. It may be useful in a large public library without open access where the only way of finding a book is by using the catalogue and copying out the shelf mark. A catalogue of a part of a collection is sometimes useful when there are many pamphlets or plays bound together in volumes and a single volume may contain works by a dozen different authors. Sermons of the seventeenth and eighteenth centuries are often preserved in this way, and some booksellers have the barbarous habit of splitting such volumes up because the pamphlets command a higher price when sold separately. This short-term gain is more than counterbalanced by the loss of durability.

If a private library is homogeneous and large enough to achieve something like completeness in its chosen field, a catalogue may be a blessing because it can become at least the nucleus of a subject bibliography. Thus the catalogues of Lord Rothschild's eighteenth-century collection and of Michael Sadleir's nineteenth-century fiction are of first importance to students in those fields.

Alphabetical arrangement is useful within certain sections of a library. A man with a large collection of English literature may begin by dividing his books according to period or genre, but when he is confronted with several yards of shelves all containing, say, English literature of the twentieth century, he may find it useful to carry out further sub-division by alphabetical order of authors' names. Such an arrangement is better than one by alphabetical order of titles, since titles are arbitrary whereas subdivision by authors brings together books that have one important feature in common and, provided that authors are not too versatile, it introduces a subject classification within the alphabetical arrangement. Similarly biographies can best be classified according to their subjects rather than their authors, since it is the subject that is more likely to be remembered or sought by a reader.

To be collectable a book needs to be complete, clean and undisturbed. While satisfying the first two qualities, many books fail in the third; pages may have been washed or replaced. Writers on collecting urge their readers to buy only copies in the finest condition. This advice is sound if the purchaser is buying simply for investment, but it leaves unanswered the question of what is to happen to those books – the vast majority – that have survived in a condition that falls short of the finest. The lack of a half-title may reduce the cost of an early nineteenth-century novel to a small fraction of that of a perfect copy, but it does not reduce its value to a research worker in a similar proportion. It would be a pity if it were to be reduced to the level of waste paper. Standards of condition vary from age to age and from country to country, and scholars collating texts may find copies useful even if they lack half-titles or some of the plates. One must distinguish according to the category to which the book belongs. A sumptuously-printed private press edition of an English classic is likely to be bought by a collector who values condition and who pays a high price for the book; the proportion of imperfect copies in existence is therefore likely to be low. But the collector of nineteenth-century children's books must be less austere. Nearly all the surviving copies of books of this kind have been roughly handled by their readers. When you are speaking of child-ren's books, it is no idle metaphor to say that their owners devoured their contents. Similarly it is silly to be too fussy about the condition of really rare books. A perfect copy of such a book may not exist or may exist only in a great national library. If this is so, imperfect copies should cer-tainly be admitted to a collection. They may provide speci-mens of early typography or engraving or, in a manuscript book of hours, the illuminations that survive may be con-sidered as self-contained individual works of art.

Condition is concerned with the handsome appearance of a book, but it is concerned even more with its purity or freedom from sophistication, or 'doctoring', which aims at concealing defects. A highly esteemed edition may have imperfect parts replaced from another, less highly esteemed, or two imperfect copies may be combined to form one that looks perfect.

Most collectors want their books to be in their original condition, as far as possible. Others seek appropriateness. If a novel is not in original boards, they would rather have it in a contemporary than a later fine binding or, if not a con-temporary binding, a contemporary style. The two qualities of original condition and appropriate binding have come to be appreciated during the present century. In the nineteenth century collectors were fond of uniform bindings, whereas today book-buyers welcome variety.

Ruskin wrote with enthusiasm about well-produced books, but he treated his library badly on the pretext that his books were there for use and not as curiosities. This argu-ment is unconvincing because it ignores the needs of future owners of the books. Some of his books, now at Bembridge in the Isle of Wight, have had their heads and tails sawn off to make them fit the shelves, and his *Hours of Yolande of Navarre* (c. 1353) has lost 37 of its leaves which he lent or gave away. It is now in the British Library as part of the Yates Thompson collection, but 13 leaves are in the Bodleian.[1] He never had more than about 4,000 books but he was constantly buying, selling and giving them away, many to the library of his Guild of St George Museum at Sheffield. At least 88 illuminated manuscripts passed through his hands, though the longest of his three lists includes only 24. Ruskin's own cataloguing of these manuscripts is so vague as to be nearly worthless. We find, for example, entries like 'Delicate small Horae of 15th century' or 'Italian best'. Ruskin bought some of the manuscripts of Sir Walter Scott's novels. His father bought the manuscript of *The Fortunes of Nigel* for £25; Hugh Walpole bought it for £400 and in 1938 presented it to his old school, King's at Canterbury.

There is a good rough and ready rule about the temperature and humidity of a room in which books are kept. Fortunately books survive best in conditions which are the most pleasant for their owners: an even temperature with a bit of a breeze blowing now and then. Collectors who live in temperate climates are fortunate in that they are spared many of the depredations from various forms of animal life that are normal in the tropics, but even in England a neglected library can crumble to dust. When John Leland visited Oxford after the suppression of the monasteries, he found few books, only moths and beetles swarming over the empty shelves. A more common fate for neglected books is that which George Bernard Shaw, in the Preface to *Cashel Byron's Profession*, records as that of the manuscript of his first novel, *Immaturity*: it was rejected by publishers and lay neglected until part of it was devoured by mice, though even they had not been able to finish it. But from the point of view of the collector partial destruction is as bad as complete disappearance, since only a few books are so highly valued that a collector would want to possess a half-eaten copy. At one university it was proposed that the publications of members of the staff should be preserved in the

1 *The Book Collector*, 1972, p. 203.

university library in dust-proof boxes; a cynical member of staff asked whether the boxes were designed to keep the dust out or in.

Dust does less harm to books than clumsy attempts to remove it. In a room with an open coal-fire the dust which settles on the top edges of books is likely to be greasy, and energetic dusting will leave a permanent stain of grease mixed with carbon. A feather-brush or one with soft bristles is less likely to leave a stain than a duster. Some book-lovers claim that books should never be dusted until they are read or consulted. This advice is sound if their owner can be satisfied that he alone will have access to them and that he will never be in such a hurry to consult a book that he will forget to dust it first. The price to be paid for neglect is that when the book is opened, a cloud of dust will rise from the top edges and settle on the newly-opened page, leaving a number of indelible spots when the book is closed again. If the dust is detected in time, it can be blown away, but the owner and his guests cannot spend all their time lightly blowing dust away.

Dr Johnson's method of dusting his books had little to recommend it. When about to dust them he drew on huge gloves, such as those once worn by hedgers and ditchers, and then, clutching his folios and octavos, he banged and buffeted them together until he was enveloped in a cloud of dust. This violent exercise over, he restored the books, all battered and bruised, to their places, where, of course, the dust resettled itself as speedily as possible.

Dust is the chief of the accidental enemies of books, but books suffer a good deal from deliberate ill-treatment by those who have not learned to respect them. Turning down the corner of a page to save the trouble of reaching for a bookmark leaves a permanent scar, and wrenching a paper-back open too far can cause the leaves to cascade onto the floor to the surprise of the offender. Readers with an interest in botany find a book a convenient flower-press, and those who collect newspaper cuttings find it a useful filing system to put a cutting, or several cuttings, within the leaves of a book of related interest. The practice of underlining passages that the reader thinks particularly important has its origin in a praiseworthy conviction that books are meant to be read and understood, but it pays no regard to the possibility that one book may be read by many different readers all with different tastes. I once read an early edition of a Victorian novel which had been heavily marked in this way and I found the markings a real help. The nineteenth-century reader had underlined all the moralizing passages and I soon found that the heavily underlined passages were just those that I wanted to skip. But whatever we do with our own books, the marking of library books is to be deprecated. A volume in one university library bears witness to the exasperation that this practice can cause. A reader had added copious notes in pencil and at one point the pencil gave way to ink. A subsequent reader added the comment: 'My God! Has he bought a fountain-pen now?'

Bookworms have caused much trouble to collectors of older books but recently-published books do not suffer very much from their activities. The partial explanation is that the bookworms are connoisseurs who do not care for the inferior paper that is used nowadays with its admixture of chemicals; they prefer a nice Caxton. Another reason for the comparative immunity of modern books is that bookworms thrive on neglected books; a modern novel that is frequently read and handled gives them no scope. It is not only the printed page that suffers; some bookworms like bindings and they are said to be fond of the paste used by binders. Several different Latin names have been given to bookworms. They may all be correct; there is no reason to suppose that any one species has exclusive rights. Holbrook Jackson mentions some[1]: one of them is *Anglossa penguinalis*, which sounds as though it ought to concentrate on paperbacks.

The prerequisite for preserving – as for repairing – a

[1] *The Anatomy of Bibliomania*, p. 553.

book is a knowledge of how the book is made in the first instance. The best preservation of a book is gentle and careful handling, which is better for the book than simply leaving it untouched. With handling there is less danger of the joints of leather-bound books becoming hard and brittle. The life of a book can be lengthened if its owner learns how to open it. When a new book is opened carelessly, one sometimes hears a loud crack and for the rest of its life the book will open most easily at the same page. The explanation is that it has been opened in the middle when it should have been laid flat on a table and then opened, a few pages at a time, from the front and the back alternately.

One of the problems faced by any collector is learning which defects matter. A stamp with an error in printing may be worth much more than a normal copy, but a badly-struck coin or a carelessly-printed book is worth less.

Bindings should not be scratched or faded. The back-strip is the most vulnerable part of the binding. If books are packed too tightly on a shelf, the top of the back-strip may be torn by careless removal. The average reader removes a book from its shelf by touching the top of the back-strip. He shouldn't. The book should be taken between thumb and fore-finger half way down the back-strip and gently withdrawn. The books should not be packed so tightly that withdrawal presents any difficulty, nor must they be so loose that they sag. Books containing a large number of pages are liable to fit loosely into their covers in course of time because of the weight of the pages. This tendency is increased if the book has inadequate support from other books on the shelf. In books bound in calf the front and back covers are liable to become detached.

Rare books are best kept in their original bindings. Books published in the eighteenth century or earlier have often been rebound and had their edges trimmed, sometimes savagely. The trimming of the edges may have been done so carelessly that the margin disappears completely and the guillotine has cut into the text. Such books have little value. A common compromise is to trim only the top edges of the page which, if left uncut, becomes a dust-trap. A book whose pages have been only slightly trimmed will be described as a 'fine tall copy' and the few extra millimetres will greatly add to its value.

The cost of early printed books has increased so enormously during the last two hundred years that we find it hard to believe how they were ill-treated. It causes us no horror to hear of newspapers being used to wrap up fish and chips and we react with amusement or derision when we hear of people who hoard every scrap of paper on which written or printed words occur in case it contains some great truth. An eighteenth-century grocer is said to have torn pages out of a Caxton as we might tear them out of an old telephone directory for wrapping-paper. The surprising thing is that indifference was not confined to the unlettered. A witness to the indifference of early collectors to the books that they collected is the Bagford collection of title-pages and fragments, formerly part of the Harley collection of manuscripts in the British Library but now transferred to the Department of Printed Books. It has been described as a typographical cemetery, a charnel-house of books crowded together without respect to their subject-matter, including a leaf of a Caxton, the title-page of *Romeus and Julietta*, on which Shakespeare's play is based, and broadsheets preserved entire.

John Bagford (1650–1716) was a founder of the Society of Antiquaries who planned to write a *History of Printing*. A shoemaker turned bookseller, he spent his spare time in amassing a collection of title-pages, emblems, prints and tail-pieces. His activities in collecting illustrative material for his never-written book have earned him the obloquy of later collectors by the extent of his depredations. He is said to have been responsible for the mutilation of 25,000 books to fill the forty-two folio volumes in which his collection is housed. The reaction of a bibliographer of today to such a collection is horror at the mutilation of priceless early printed books that must have taken place to produce it, but Bagford's defenders have pointed out that much of his material was taken from volumes that were already imperfect and that the material that he mutilated was in his day universally neglected. Moreover, but for him, many books of which we have now some evidence would have perished completely.

Similar feelings must be aroused by the sight of a single book swollen out to fill a dozen or more volumes by the insertion of additional illustrations. In the eighteenth and nineteenth centuries large sums were spent on the production of these mammoth collections. The term 'grangerizing' is used because James Granger (1723–1776) collected fourteen thousand engraved portraits, and his *Biographical History of England* was a favourite choice for extra-illustrators. A grangerized book is sometimes described as fit only for a vandal's library.

What seems vandalism to one collector may seem admirable to another. One bookseller prepared a few copies of *Pickwick Papers* containing every plate in every state. They sold well, but one must spare a thought for the mutilated remnants of copies of the book, lacking some of the plates, which the bookseller's activities have left strewn in various bookshops throughout the world.

The grangerizer should not become too ambitious. Two rules will keep the damage that he does within bounds. He should choose his material only from books that are already imperfect or from unbound periodicals which are unlikely to survive, and he should not dismember the book that he is extra-illustrating, but keep his illustrations, mounted on sheets of uniform size in spring-back folders by the side of the book that he is illustrating. He may well choose a book like Garnett and Gosse's four-volume *History of English Literature* that is already well illustrated.

Those who feel tempted to grangerize may be able to sublimate the desire by building up a collection of illustrations. The value of such a collection in the study of geography or the history of art is obvious, and there are many subjects which could be made more vivid by a greater use of visual aids. What was a harmful activity of rich collectors can thus become a comparatively harmless activity of impecunious bibliophiles. Even more harmless, because the raw material is more expendable, is the building up of a collection of newspaper cuttings. These can be mounted on quarto leaves and each cutting given a Dewey classification number as though it were a book. Such a collection can be made at no cost at all. The chief danger is that it can easily become so large as to be unmanageable, and the collector of newspaper cuttings would be wise to specialize in a very limited field.

In the days when a private library was a large room lined with books, some collectors were inclined to resent the presence of a door. It was not that the space was needed for books, but any gap in the neat row of shelves was considered a blemish. To conceal it the practice grew up of fitting the door with dummy shelves on which were placed dummy books, often with facetious titles. Dickens had such a library and he enjoyed thinking up titles for the dummy books. The sixth Duke of Devonshire, wanting to construct a door of this kind for the library staircase at Chatsworth, asked Thomas Hood to suggest a few titles. Hood was a good man for the job, for there is a tradition of punning in the choice of dummy titles, and Hood was a notorious punster. Among the titles he suggested were Lamb's *Reflections on Suet*, Malthus's *Attack on Infantry*, John Knox *On Death's Door*, Boyle *On Steam*, *The Scottish Boccaccio* by D. Cameron, and *Cursory Remarks on Swearing*.

A legitimate reason for wanting to destroy evidence of ownership is that a book may contain an inscription showing that it was presented by the author and its sale might seem to reveal ingratitude. End-papers are sometimes ripped out, and even title-pages may go. However, there has probably been an improvement in the standards of the care of books during the last four centuries.

In the early years of the twentieth century books were often published in cloth with a paper label on the spine giving the title. Publishers realized that such labels were fragile and issued duplicate labels, lightly stuck on one of the back end-papers. Is a book complete if the original paper label has been discarded and replaced by this duplicate?

If a name written in a book is the author's, most collectors would think that it added to the value of the book, although there is a sad story that one second-hand book was advertised: 'Without the usual presentation inscription from the author. Rare in this condition.' If the name is that of a well-known person, it adds to the value of the book, converting it into an 'association copy'. If the name is unknown, it is best that it should be unobtrusive, neat and not on the title-page.

At one time publishers used to stamp 'For review' or 'Presentation copy' in review copies in order to discourage reviewers from selling them. The practice is no longer common because it estranged reviewers and did not serve its purpose. Some people claim that such a stamp enhances the value of the book by making it clear that it is the first issue if there is more than one, but most people would probably regard it as a blemish. Large numbers of books of little value are sent out for review but are never reviewed. These are generally sold in bulk to second-hand booksellers. It is not a commendation of a book to be associated with lots that are so unattractive that, so far as the evidence goes, no one has loved them well enough to pay any money for them.

Books with perfectly genuine signatures have often been mass-produced, especially in the present century. An author will turn up at a bookshop as part of a promotion campaign and sign copies of his book for any purchaser without extra charge. The American poet Robert Frost gave a reading of his poems at a women's college and provided a printed text, thinking that it would help the students to follow him. It was a kindly thought, but the experiment was not repeated, because he was virtually swamped by autograph seekers waving the leaflets before his startled eyes and demanding his signature.

The most valuable kind of association copy is one annotated by the author. One that is highly valued, though naturally rarely found, is the dedication copy presented by the author to the person to whom it is dedicated. Next come books which once belonged to someone particularly associated with the contents of the book. Books bearing the signature of a well-known man who had no connection with the author or subject of the book are less valuable. Authors' signatures in ink are more valuable than those in pencil and full names are better than initials. Most well-known authors receive presentation copies of books from minor authors with the eminent man's name in the handwriting of the donor. These have little value; a book presented by its famous author to a nonentity is more valuable. If an inscription is dated, it may have added value. Most valuable is a book with an inscription to a named recipient at or near the date of publication; next in value is a book with an undated inscription or with a date much later than the date of publication; last comes a book with the inscription 'From the author' instead of a signature. A book with an autograph letter inserted or 'laid in' is not really an association copy. Such a book is two items: a book and an autograph letter. It is worthy of the attention of a collector if the letter refers to the book in question.

Books that are inscribed by the author in response to an owner's request are less valuable than presentation copies. Some authors were more ready than others to inscribe their books. Gissing and Meredith rarely did so and books bearing their signatures are therefore valuable. Tennyson, Browning and Dickens were very free with inscriptions but Thackeray and Matthew Arnold were not.[1] Scott often inscribed his poems, but an inscribed copy of one of his novels would naturally arouse a collector's suspicions. A. E. Housman hardly ever refused to sign a copy of one of his books but he sent out very few presentation copies. Consequently signed

[1] John Carter, *Taste and Technique in Book-Collecting*, p. 87.

copies of his books are plentiful but presentation copies with an inscription are rare.

Every book-collector has to decide what to do about borrowers. I think that we are too indulgent to them. They have been spoilt by the services provided by public libraries, and they get into the way of thinking that they are doing us a favour by borrowing our books. It is all very well to have a book-plate saying that a book belongs to Grolier and his friends, but the man who adopts this practice is liable to find, like the man who relies on a public library, that when he wants a book, it is out. One collector was praising a book to a friend, who innocently asked if he might borrow it. The collector replied indignantly: 'Certainly not. I will show you the reason when you next come to see me.' When the visitor called and asked the reason, the collector opened a door and revealed a roomful of books, saying: 'There you are. Every one of them borrowed.'

This is not borrowing; it is theft. The ethics of borrowing are rather different. Everyone, of course, has a right to borrow whenever he can find a willing lender, but it is well to consider what would be the result if people were to buy more books instead of borrowing them. The short answer is that it would send up the prices of old books and send down the prices of new ones. The supply of old books is fixed, so any increase in demand will inevitably raise the price, but the effect of an increase in the number of purchasers of new books would be that publishers could print larger, and therefore cheaper, editions.

CHAPTER V

TRENDS IN BOOK-COLLECTING

BOOK-COLLECTING is very much influenced by fashion,
which has its effect on the esteem enjoyed by the pursuit as a whole and on the attention paid to particular
fields. Changes in fashion are reflected in the references to
particular subjects in the literature of the time, but we have
to remember that subjects that appeal to literary critics are not
necessarily those that are of interest to collectors, and a better
measure of the popularity of a subject or an author with collectors is a record of the prices at which books in a particular
field have been sold. The history of rises and falls in the prices
of books is a proper subject of study for the collector, but it is
a painful one, because it is a history of lost opportunities. On
the other hand the elderly collector can derive satisfaction
from reflecting how cheaply he bought books that are sold at
high prices today. If he traces prices over a period of a century
or more, the changes that he discovers may be startling. Long
runs of *The Gentleman's Magazine* were once described as
'decisively unsaleable', but a run of 235 volumes was sold in
1968 for £680. Like most growth, the rate of increase has not
been constant. Prices move in a succession of steps, and some
of the steps lead downward, but the history of the price of any
book can undergo a series of sudden jumps. The fluctuations
in price are comparable with those of stocks and shares and,
since rare books are increasingly bought for investment, the
prices of books and those of shares often march hand in hand.
Percy Muir, with wide experience as a bookseller, wrote:

Anyone well informed on book-collecting history could venture a shrewd guess at the state of the money-market from the current price of a Kelmscott Chaucer.[1]

The famous bookseller A. S. W. Rosenbach was fond of insisting that rare books are a good investment. He wrote:

> I know many a captain of industry who quietly hides away in the secrecy of his strong box rare little volumes, such as Shakespeare quartos, small pamphlets by Shelley, and even first editions of Joseph Conrad. These rich men realize – and rightly, too – that such treasure will always sell at a premium, even though the market is tumbling and Wall Street is in a panic . . . Their volumes can be sent to the auction mart at any time, where they will realize, as a rule, their full value.[2]

The tone of this comment will jar on many collectors but, more important, it is an exaggeration. Anyone who buys rare books as an investment should realize that the time when he is most likely to want to sell his books is the time when he is least likely to get a good price for them. Without too much exaggeration one can envisage a time when the collector offers his Kelmscott Chaucer to a man who says that what he really wants is a tin of baked beans. Only a very optimistic collector would expect to sell his books for their full value when Wall Street was in a panic.

It is now generally known that old books can be valuable, but one of the chief trials of a second-hand bookseller is the widespread belief that all old books must be valuable. Newspaper publicity about the high price paid for such a book as the first edition of *Pilgrim's Progress* produces a string of optimists on their way to booksellers with nineteenth-century editions which they have found in attics and which must be worth their weight in gold. Such offers are among the burdens that a successful bookseller has to carry. On a single day

[1] P. H. Muir, *Book-Collecting as a Hobby in a Series of Letters to Everyman* (Gramol Publications, 1944), p. 57.
[2] A. S. W. Rosenbach, *Books and Bidders* (George Allen, 1927), pp. 79 f.

Rosenbach received 275 offers of books for sale, and he esti-
mated that the proportion of worthwhile material was one
third of one per cent.

Prices depend in the main on variations in supply and
demand, but they can respond to other influences. It is possible
to recognize some of the reasons why a decline in prices may
take place, and a far-sighted collector can avoid the financial
loss involved in buying at the top of the market if he learns to
recognize some of the causes of a forthcoming decline. One
reason why a field of collecting may cease to be fashionable
or may never become so is lack of material. In certain fields
most of the surviving books are now in public libraries, and
the few copies that remain in private hands fetch fantastic
prices when they do come on the market. The collector of
limited means knows that they are not for him and turns to
other fields. Another reason for loss of esteem is exactly the
opposite: if there is too much material collectors feel that
there is no point in buying books that are never likely to command high prices, or they may think that the field is so large
that they are never likely to achieve the completeness that is
one of the aims of the collector. Then again, the publication
of a bibliography may work in either of two directions. If the
bibliography aims at completeness and numbers the items, it
encourages demand among those collectors whose approach
is that of the stamp-collector. A collector who has Numbers
30 and 32 will want Number 31. A bibliography which has
had this effect is A. W. Pollard and G. R. Redgrave's *A Short
Title Catalogue of Books Printed in England, Scotland, and
Ireland and of English Books Printed Abroad 1475–1640*, published by the Bibliographical Society in 1926. But a detailed
bibliography may have the opposite effect of making the
collector lose heart when he discovers that he has chosen a
complicated field that he has no chance of covering completely. This has happened with the novels of Sir Walter
Scott. Greville Worthington's bibliography has revealed so
many variants that collectors have learnt to be rather afraid of
Scott, and consequently first editions of his novels can be

bought comparatively cheaply. Furthermore, the market may be artificially stimulated by the production of catalogues with high prices designed to persuade collectors that books in a particular category are valuable, and a bookseller with a good stock of books in a particular field has an interest in seeing that books in that field do not publicly change hands at low prices. Most booksellers have their favourite fields and, more usefully to the impecunious book-buyer, fields that they dislike. The wealthy collector will go to the specialist book-seller who is most likely to have a good stock but whose prices are high. The impoverished collector will go to a larger num-ber of shops and will get the best bargains from booksellers whose tastes differ from his own. On the death of an author the prices of his books tend to fall. If the author is a nonentity whose books have been sold at inflated prices, the fall will be permanent, but if he has real merit there will be a slow revival. Other influences can dampen the enthusiasm of individual col-lectors without affecting the market as a whole. For example, when a collection stops growing, its owner tends to lose inter-est in it. Two influences which can cause a collector to turn to other fields or to stop collecting altogether are the publication of a catalogue of his collection and the provision of a hand-some building to house it.

In spite of fluctuations for special reasons such as these, there are many records to show that some books highly valued today were once little regarded by either booksellers or collectors. Wilmarth Lewis, the well-known collector of material relating to Horace Walpole, records his experiences:

I have been told by old-time booksellers that before there was a market for any book from Walpole's library, they thought little of pulping unimportant books formerly in it that were in poor condition. The bookplate was always worth half a crown. The dealers soaked it off and either sold it separately or pasted it into another book. They stripped off the covers and threw the book into a sack, which they sold for half a sovereign when it was filled. The covers, with the precious shelf-marks, went into the office fire.[1]

It is interesting to note that an increase of interest in the books once possessed by a well-known man of letters has been accompanied by a decline of interest in book-plates. Lewis's booksellers could sell a book-plate for half a crown while the book in which it was pasted was worthless, whereas today book-plates do not arouse much interest, perhaps from a realization that it is easy to transfer them from one book to another, and they therefore do not give reliable evidence of ownership.

Speculators can cause fluctuations in the prices of books, but their influence is not entirely harmful. When the idea gets about that there is money in books, old books have a better chance of preservation. In the hope of making a profit, many people are induced to buy worthless books that they believe to be worth a fortune, but among the rubbish there may be a few valuable books that would have been destroyed but for the publicity given to high prices. Trouble lies ahead if the speculators, with no interest in the contents of books, all unload their holdings at the same time.

The prices of new books present different problems. Older book-buyers are shocked at the high prices at which new books are published today, but younger buyers take these prices in their stride, because they have known nothing better. Prices seem high because in the first half of the present century we had got used to very low prices for books both new and second-hand. This is true not so much of 'collectors' items' as of the general run of books that can be published in large editions. When nearly a thousand volumes in 'Everyman's Library' were in print at two shillings a volume and when most of them could be bought second-hand for ninepence, there were few recreations so cheap as reading, even if one never used a lending library. We are now emerging from a

---

[1] *Collector's Progress*, p. 114.

period of low prices, and cheap books have suffered more than the highly-priced. Many cheap editions are now ten times the price that they used to be, whereas 'coffee-table books' have not risen in price to the same extent.

The early British collectors brought together huge collections of miscellaneous books which eventually developed into great university or national libraries. Thus the collection of Sir Thomas Bodley (1545–1613) formed the nucleus of the Bodleian at Oxford and that of Sir Hans Sloane (1660–1753) was the basis on which the British Library was built. Some famous collections have remained intact, encapsulated in large institutional libraries. Such collections are those of John Moore (1646–1714), Bishop of Ely, in Cambridge University Library, of Sir Robert Cotton (1571–1631) in the British Library, of the second Earl Spencer (1758–1834) in the John Rylands Library of the University of Manchester, and of Thomas Jefferson (1743–1826) in the Library of Congress at Washington. Garrick's plays and Malone's Shakespearean collection went to the British Museum, later to become the British Library. This sort of thing still goes on, but the size of the great national libraries tends to discourage it. Collectors fear that their books would be lost in the immensity of an institution like the British Library.

Some information about the interests of early collectors can be gathered from book auction catalogues, many of which have been preserved. Among them are catalogues of the libraries of well-known men of letters. These have naturally attracted the attention of literary historians, but to draw conclusions about the reading of a man of letters from the auction catalogue of his library is a perilous proceeding, because it was always possible for a bookseller to slip in extra volumes from other sources in order to profit from the publicity conferred by the name of an eminent owner. Moreover, books were often offered in lots of fifty or more volumes out of which only one or two titles might be quoted. But from a large number of catalogues a few general conclusions are possible.

In the course of the eighteenth century we can see that theology attracted less attention while travel and modern literature received more. In a typical eighteenth-century library there will be a good range of the classics, a large number of books of travel, a wide range of British and French literature, and some books in Italian and Spanish but not many in German. Other fields well represented are memoirs, topography, natural history and art.

A book acquires added interest by having formed a part of a famous collection, even if the collection is afterwards dispersed, and the respect which collectors show for provenance has had an interesting linguistic result in creating some very long strings of proper names used to record previous ownership in a single sentence, such as 'the Jerome Kern-Anderson Galleries-Rosenbach-Owen. D. Young-Gabriel Wells-Rothschild copy' of *Tom Jones* (6 vols., 1749).[1]

Some British kings have been great collectors, and some of their collections have been preserved, giving to posterity a good picture of the taste of the times and providing splendid examples of the art of bookbinding. In 1759 George II presented to the British Museum the Old Royal Library, some of whose books dated from the reign of Henry VII. Many of these books were rebound in a uniform style after they came to the British Museum. When George III came to the throne, he began to build up a fine collection at Buckingham House. George IV employed Nash to remodel the Palace, as it had become, and found the books in the way, so they came to the British Museum in 1823, forming the King's Library. William IV inherited shelves empty except for thirty of the finest of George II's books, which had been excepted from his gift, and he built up the Windsor Castle Library and entailed it so that it could not be given to the nation.

In the early nineteenth century book-collecting was an aristocratic activity, and this approach is still preserved in the list of the forty members printed in each of the publications

---

[1] John Carter, *Taste and Technique in Book-Collecting*, p. 53.

of the Roxburghe Club, with one name printed in red to indicate the ownership of that particular volume. In a typical list of members half the number are peers, while the rest are baronets, knights or eminent collectors. Early nineteenth-century collectors were especially interested in early printing and book illustration and editions of the classics. It was during this period that some of the great country-house libraries were being built up. There are many such libraries today, but they are for the most part survivals from the past, since we are more mobile than our ancestors and we generally have smaller houses. The removal of a large number of books from one house to another presents a number of quite severe practical problems. It limits the choice of a house and it gives the men who handle the books a task more serious than they expected when they embarked on it.

Some of the finest private libraries have been built up over several generations, but a single break in the chain of collectors can lead to dispersal. No great harm is done to a library if an heir with no interest in books allows it to be untended for a generation, but a library may be dispersed if the heir has other expensive interests. Such a dispersal took place in 1925 when Sir George Holford, who had inherited an outstanding library, acquired an interest in the expensive hobby of growing orchids.[1]

In the later nineteenth century there began a trend away from the mammoth general collection towards the 'cabinet' collection in a limited field, of which the best example is Frederick Locker-Lampson's Rowfant Library. Interest in early printed books and bindings was maintained by some collectors, but others were interested in first editions of English literature from Chaucer to the nineteenth century. Henry Buxton Forman (1842–1917) made the Romantics fashionable, and Thomas James Wise (1859–1937) did the same for later nineteenth-century authors. Both Forman and

---

[1] Edwin Wolf and John F. Fleming, *Rosenbach: A Biography* (Weidenfeld & Nicolson, 1960), p. 221.

Wise encouraged an interest in the minor pamphlets of major authors. They were pioneers in taking an interest in English literature after the Elizabethan period and, as pioneers, they were able to pick up unfashionable rarities cheaply. They developed a technique of getting in touch with the relatives and friends of authors recently dead in order to buy association material, especially manuscripts, which might have been destroyed but for their efforts. After the death of Swinburne in 1909 Wise succeeded in buying almost the entire contents of Number 2, The Pines, Putney, where the poet spent the last thirty years of his life. From Leigh Hunt's daughter he bought the copy of *Epipsychidion* that Shelley had given to her father, and he also bought books from George Borrow's daughter. His friend Clement Shorter bought a lot of Brontë material from Charlotte Brontë's widower, the Rev. A. B. Nicholls, and he divided the spoils with Wise. By opening up new fields, Wise made book-collecting possible for comparatively poor collectors. He produced many bibliographies, which included statements about the priority of issues and editions that encouraged a growing interest in bibliography. There was among collectors a growing conviction of the importance of original condition, encouraged by the detailed description of the physical characteristics of books in author bibliographies. Wise reinforced his precepts as a bibliographer by his practice as a collector; he was willing to pay high prices for copies in boards or original wrappers. He is best known today for his activities as a forger, which are discussed in a later chapter, and he was able to dispose of his forgeries because of a new trend of which he took advantage: the rise of the amateur dealer. Before his time collectors, who were usually well-to-do and lightly taxed, felt that to mention a book's price was in rather bad taste. Wise and his friends took a good deal of interest in prices and sold books as well as buying them. This change in attitude was in part the result of specialization, and the trend has continued into the present century. Without conscious effort collectors acquire some knowledge of books that they do not themselves want to possess and, in browsing in bookshops, they find many bargains outside their own special fields. It is natural that they should sometimes pick up these bargains with a view to resale.

During the twentieth century there has been an increased interest in the work of living authors. The taste of collectors has lagged behind that of literary critics, and old-fashioned modern authors remained for some time in vogue with collectors. John Carter[1] points out that James Joyce's *Ulysses* (Paris, 1922) remained unsaleable at a tenth of the price of J. M. Barrie's *My Lady Nicotine* (1890). Middle-brow novelists, like H. G. Wells and Arnold Bennett, appealed more strongly to readers than to collectors but D. H. Lawrence was popular with collectors.

In the twentieth century specialization became more common, although there were some survivors of the wide-ranging collectors of the past, including Sir Leicester Harmsworth, one of the many younger brothers of Viscount Northcliffe, of whom an envious fellow-collector said that he made *The Cambridge Bibliography of English Literature* his preliminary finding-list when making purchases.

Until the 1920s there was little general interest in the eighteenth century, although a few outstanding authors, like Fielding, Boswell and Johnson, were collected. In the 1920s there was a revival of interest, which owed a good deal to the booksellers trading under the name of Elkin Mathews who, in 1925, issued a catalogue of books relating to Dr Johnson in which books of that period were offered at high prices; the confidence of the booksellers proved infectious and spread to collectors. Likewise, the writings of Michael Sadleir, as critic and bibliographer, did much to encourage an interest in the novels of Anthony Trollope.

Since the Second World War the most noticeable development has been an increased interest in early scientific literature. Collectors no longer confined their attention to English literature but sought to acquire first editions of landmarks in

[1] op. cit. p. 47.

the history of thought. One of the best-known collectors in this field was John Maynard Keynes (1843–1946), afterwards Lord Keynes, elder brother of the eminent bibliographer Sir Geoffrey Keynes. High prices were paid for illustrated books of the eighteenth and early nineteenth centuries, especially if they contained botanical illustrations, which appealed to collectors in more than one field. In earlier centuries there had been occasional pioneers like George Thomason (d. 1666), who realized the value that ephemera might have for scholars in the future; Thomason's collection of nearly 23,000 Civil War Tracts was presented to the British Museum by George III in 1762. During the twentieth century interest in such material has become more general. An important collection in this field was that formed by John Johnson, who was for many years Printer to the Oxford University Press. His test for inclusion was that an object should illustrate some aspect of the history of printing. The collection therefore contains many things that are not generally collected, such as company prospectuses and cotton-reel labels.

During the present century American collectors have been of outstanding importance. Chief among them were Pierpont Morgan, Henry Huntington and Henry Folger, who concentrated respectively on early printing, English literature and Shakespeare, though they shared the wide-ranging tastes of the early British collectors. At first American collectors had been chiefly attracted by English books, but during the twentieth century they have shown an increasing interest in Americana.

CHAPTER VI

SOME GREAT COLLECTORS

I N medieval England the great libraries were those of the
monasteries, which were dispersed at the time of Henry
VIII. A few collectors salvaged what they could from the
wreck of the libraries, and one of them, Matthew Parker
(1504–75), Archbishop of Canterbury, bequeathed 433 manuscripts to Corpus Christi College, Cambridge. One of the
most important collections of early manuscripts is that formed
by Sir Robert Cotton (1571–1631), who was educated at
Winchester, where his antiquarian interests were encouraged
by William Camden, the second master. He sided with
parliamentary reformers and was brought before the Star
Chamber, but the birth of the future Charles II on the date
fixed for his trial secured him an amnesty. After his death his
library was kept in Ashburnham House, Westminster, where
it was badly damaged by fire in 1731. Out of 958 manuscripts
114 were destroyed or badly damaged and in 1753 the surviving manuscripts became part of the newly founded British
Museum. Cotton arranged his books in fourteen bookcases
with a bust of a Roman emperor above each case. The name of
the emperor provided the first element in the shelf-mark and
these shelf-marks are still used. A typical shelf-mark is Cotton
Caligula A. ix. The Cotton collection contains our chief or
only texts of some of the masterpieces of medieval literature,
including *Beowulf* and *Sir Gawain and the Green Knight*.

The chief interest of Samuel Pepys (1633–1703) during his
early manhood was his Diary; in his later years it was his
Library, which remains to this day in Magdalene College,
Cambridge, a monument to his intense love of his own

possessions and his passion for methodical arrangement. He saw to it that it exactly filled twelve handsome glazed book-cases. The books are arranged with extreme neatness, most of the shelves having double rows with folios at the back and smaller books at the front. They are arranged by size rather than subject, but if any books in a series are shorter than the rest, they have been provided with wooden supports, gilded to imitate the backs of the volumes, to bring them up to the right level. They are numbered consecutively from 1 to 3,000, bound in dark-brown calf, the backs gilded and the sides stamped with Pepys's arms. Each volume has two book-plates, one of them bearing an engraved portrait of Pepys.

The most important of the contents of the Library is the manuscript of Pepys's Diary in six volumes. Of the three thousand volumes in the Library about two hundred and fifty are manuscripts, some medieval but most of them belonging to Pepys's own day. Many of the manuscripts reflect Pepys's interest in music and naval affairs. There are over a hundred volumes of naval papers, many of them copies that had been made for Pepys but some of them originals, which he had kept without having an undeniable right to do so. The Library contains an important collection of State papers for which their owner John Evelyn had been looking everywhere. He had lent them to Pepys, who kept them in spite of requests for their return. A document of historical interest is the original list of the provisions carried by the Spanish Armada in 1588, bound in vellum boards and pierced with a hole by which to hang it up. Early printed books, such as those of Caxton and Wynkyn de Worde, are well represented. In choosing such books Pepys relied on the advice of friends, but in choosing the pamphlets and news-letters of his own time he relied on his own judgement, and he had a good eye for what was worth preserving. He was ahead of his time in realizing the importance to the historian of ephemera. His collection of eighteen hundred broadside ballads bound in five folio volumes is said to be the largest in existence, and some of the imposing bound volumes in his collection have such titles as

Penny Merriments and *Penny Godlinesses*. Plays and books of travel are well represented, as well as books in French, Spanish and Italian. There are scrap-books containing maps, engravings and fragments of medieval manuscripts. Two of these fragments have a note that they were presented to Pepys by his honoured friends the Dean and Chapter of Durham and they have been neatly cut from the pages of two books still to be seen in the Chapter Library at Durham, an instance of the lack of attention paid to the conservation of medieval manuscripts in the seventeenth century. A similar indifference to condition has had the result that many of the engraved portraits are shorn of their margins.

The arrangements which Pepys made for the disposal of his library have become famous as an example of ingenuity in devising precautions against the shortcomings of librarians. His nephew John Jackson was required to check the collection to see that nothing was missing and to complete any series that might still be in course of publication. Two Cambridge colleges, Trinity and Magdalene, were to have 'a reciprocal check upon one another', the college in possession of the library to be subject to an annual visitation from the other and to forfeit the whole collection if Pepys's directions for its safe keeping were disregarded. Fortunately this direction did not result in an annual transfer of the collection from one college to the other; there is no record to show that Trinity ever paid it the stipulated visits of inspection.[1]

George John, second Earl Spencer (1758–1834) did much to build up the Althorp Library, founded by his ancestor Charles Spencer, third Earl of Sunderland (1674–1722). His father, the first Earl Spencer, a collector in a small way, had bought the collection of 5,000 volumes formed by William George, Principal of Eton, including a number of Elizabethan pamphlets which were absorbed in the collection of the second Earl. The Althorp collection first became important

---

[1] See Percy Lubbock, *Samuel Pepys* (Nelson n.d.), pp. 256–80.

with the acquisition of the collection of Count Reviczky, a Hungarian nobleman, whose collection was particularly strong in editions of the Greek and Latin classics. Reviczky attached great importance to condition and had a hatred of books with manuscript notes, however eminent the annotator. In 1790 he sold his library to Spencer for £1,000 down and an annuity of £500. Three years later he died and Lord Spencer had acquired an outstanding collection on bargain terms.

In 1807 Spencer retired from official life and for the next thirty years devoted his chief attention to the building up of his library. In 1802 he became friendly with Thomas Frognall Dibdin, to whom he afterwards entrusted the care of his library. Spencer was never afraid of selling duplicates and, after picking out the gems and finer copies of books that he already had, he sent the rest for sale by auction. With the passage of time libraries often find themselves in possession of older books that have enormously increased in value while they are short of money to buy more modern books. Spencer was always ready to negotiate with such libraries and three of the rarest of the Spencer Caxtons were obtained in this way.

Spencer continued Reviczky's attention to condition and his collection is unusually fine. It is especially important for the number of books it has which illustrate the origin and development of the art of printing. There are more than three thousand volumes printed before the year 1501. There are examples of block-printing, which preceded printing from movable types. Most of these are undated, but one, representing St Christopher, bears the date 1423, showing that it is the earliest known piece of European printing to which an unquestioned date is attached. There are fifteen block-books made up from single leaves printed on one side of the paper and pasted back to back. There are copies of the Bamberg and Mazarin Bibles and the Mainz Psalter of 1457. Books printed in Italy in the fifteenth century are well represented: they include the first edition of Boccaccio's *Il Decamerone* printed by Valdarfer in 1471. As examples of

English printing there are sixty Caxtons, of which thirty-six are perfect. Of four of these the Spencer collection has the only known copies.

An illustration of the richness of the collections of foreign literature is provided by the Dante collection of more than six thousand volumes. In English literature there are two sets of the four folios of Shakespeare and a copy of the fourth edition of Dr Johnson's *Dictionary*, with corrections by the author, which formerly belonged to Sir Joshua Reynolds.

In 1892 the fifth Earl Spencer (1835–1910) decided to sell the Althorp Library, stipulating that a purchaser should be found for the collection as a whole. It happened very fortunately that the John Rylands Library in Deansgate, Manchester was then being built and Mrs Rylands bought the collection for the Library, where it was joined in 1907 by the collection of six thousand manuscripts belonging to the Earl of Crawford, and now forms part of the Library of the University of Manchester.

Richard Heber (1773–1833), the half-brother of Bishop Reginald Heber, was one of the original members of the Roxburghe Club. He began by collecting the classics, but was a pioneer in collecting early English poetry and drama. His collection contained two to three hundred thousand volumes, which filled two houses in London, one in Oxford and several on the Continent. The disposal of his books, in sixteen sales, was a financial disaster for his family. The books sold in London had cost over £100,000 but were sold at £56,774, because the sales happened to take place between two generations of book-collectors: those who founded the Roxburghe Club and the American collectors who dominated the scene at the end of the century. The Adams sale in 1931 was a disappointment because it took place at a time of slump.

Alexander Dyce's editions of Elizabethan dramatists were based on copies that Heber had lent him. Heber was very active in persuading the Government to acquire the library of George III. The Britwell (see below) and Huth collections

included many books from Heber's library. Many of his
purchases never came to England, for they were warehoused
at Antwerp and elsewhere on the Continent, and he died, at
the age of sixty, before assimilating them to his collection.

William Henry Miller (1789–1848) was a Scotsman who
formed a library, rich in early English and Scottish literature,
at Britwell Court in Buckinghamshire and the house gave its
name to the library. Sydney Richardson Christie-Miller
inherited the Britwell Library in 1898 and sold it in 1916.
Sotheby's prepared an auction catalogue of the Americana
but the 346 lots were sold *en bloc* to Henry E. Huntington.
The Britwell Sales continued until 1927 and realized half a
million pounds.

Sir Thomas Phillipps (1792–1872) was the world's greatest
collector of manuscripts. Just as Cotton rescued manuscripts
dispersed at the dissolution of the English monasteries,
Phillipps collected the manuscripts dispersed from French and
German monasteries and private collections during the
Napoleonic Wars. His great achievement was not in his
illuminated manuscripts and other great treasures, though
there are plenty of those, but in the vast quantity of run-of-
the-mill manuscripts which would have been destroyed but
for him.

   Phillipps inherited an income of about £8,000 a year from
his father, but such was his hunger for manuscripts that for
virtually the whole of his life he was in debt. In 1822 he and
his wife resorted to the time-honoured expedient of going to
live on the Continent where living expenses were lower than
they were in England, but the move made his financial difficulties worse, since the decade after the Napoleonic wars was
a period when there were unprecedented opportunities for
the purchase of books on the Continent. Monastic libraries
had been dispersed and the market was flooded with printed
books and manuscripts offered at prices that Phillipps could
not resist.

Phillipps was a quarrelsome and niggardly man, always ready with some complicated scheme to avoid paying his employees and booksellers their due. He paid his debts with post-dated bills after much wrangling, but the sheer quantity of his purchases made booksellers put up with a lot of nonsense from him. He was always reluctant to agree to a settlement by arbitration because 'arbitrators almost always favour Tradesmen more than Gentlemen'. He clearly rejected the alternative explanation that the reason why arbitrators decided against him was that he was usually in the wrong. The following is a typical letter written to a bookseller after an auction sale:

Mr. Thorpe
    Your man had the impudence to bid against me to day . . . & if you bid against me tomorrow, I intend never to deal with you again.
    If you bought the other Hebrew Bibles at this days sale with the hope of selling them to me, I beg to say I will not have them.
I am Sir
Yours
Thos Phillipps[1]

Although the prevailing tone of Phillipps's letters is unpleasant, he sometimes shows himself in a more attractive light. He took a lot of trouble to help those who shared his scholarly interests and, until he quarrelled with them, he was capable of warm feelings towards his friends. One of them was Sir Frederic Madden, a distinguished scholar and Keeper of the Department of Manuscripts of the British Museum. In 1841 Phillipps agreed to be godfather to Madden's infant son and sent the child a copy of *The Catalogue of the Cottonian Manuscripts* as a christening present. There is nothing like starting them young. His contemporaries expressed surprise

---

[1] A. N. L. Munby, *The Formation of the Phillipps Library up to the Year 1840* (CUP, 1954), p. 55.

that Phillipps could never be persuaded to publish any account of the outstanding items in his collection, but his reluctance is adequately explained by its size. He was so bent on acquisition, sometimes buying whole libraries at a stroke, that he had no time to handle, let alone read, all the books that he bought. His private vice has turned out to be a public benefit, since many of the manuscripts that he bought, now known to be important, would have been destroyed but for his wholesale acquisitions.

Phillipps was a publisher as well as a collector. At his home he established a private press, called the Middle Hill Press for the publication of scholarly works. The printers that he employed were under-paid and had to beg for their meagre pittance. They were paid at piece-work rates and Phillipps made no attempt to provide them with continuous work. In 1842 the printer complained that he had received only £1 from his employer during the previous two months but he had to pay Phillipps £20 a year rent for the house in which he lived. In engaging a new printer Phillipps wrote:

I must have my Printer entirely under my control . . . I want a Printer who will work early & late.

To another he wrote:

I shall not like your visiting the villages here, as very little good, but a great deal of mischief is done, when that is the case.[1]

The sales of Phillipps's privately-printed publications were very small. His unfortunate booksellers had to take some of them in part-exchange for his purchases, and of many of his publications only twenty-five copies were issued. A bookseller gave him the hint that the reason for his small sales were that his books were expensive and badly produced.

[1] A. N. L. Munby, *The Formation of the Phillipps Library from 1841 to 1872* (CUP, 1956), p. 45.

Phillipps had little sympathy with those who did not share his interests. He behaved so outrageously that he became a sort of Dick Deadeye of the Victorian world of learning, and any proposal that he made was liable to be ignored or ridiculed. At the British Museum Anthony Panizzi, the Principal Librarian, and Sir Frederic Madden, the Keeper of Manuscripts, forgot their mutual animosity in order to get together and have a good laugh about twelve suggestions that Phillipps, as a Trustee, had made for the improvement of the Library. Some of the suggestions were, in fact, very sensible and included such proposals as the revision of the catalogues of the Harley and Cotton collections and the insertion of a label inside each manuscript stating where an edition of the text was to be found.

Phillipps had two particular hatreds: the Roman Catholic Church and his son-in-law James Orchard Halliwell, on whom his estate was entailed. Phillipps's house, Middle Hill, had to go to Halliwell on his death, and he therefore bought Thirlstaine House in Cheltenham and stripped Middle Hill of its trees and the lead from the roof. On his death his library and Thirlstaine House passed to his younger daughter Katharine and her husband the Rev. John Fenwick. Phillipps's will stipulated that neither his elder daughter nor her husband Halliwell nor any Roman Catholic should be allowed to have access to the library. The books were a burden to Fenwick since there was no money for their upkeep. Sales began in 1886 and are still going on. In 1945 the trustees accepted an offer of £100,000 for the whole remaining collection from the booksellers Lionel and Philip Robinson, who obtained a bargain.

Most collectors are content to build up their collections by visits to bookshops, by the armchair reading of catalogues or by the purchase of entire collections. Robert Curzon differed from these collectors in that he preferred to travel in remote parts of the world in search of manuscripts in monastic libraries and he left a record of his adventures in a minor classic *Visits to Monasteries in the Levant* (1849). He was born in 1810, the grandson of the first Viscount Curzon. His mother was in her own right Baroness Zouche, and Robert succeeded to her title, becoming fourteenth Baron Zouche in 1870, three years before his death. He became an M.P. at the age of 21 for a borough which was disfranchised by the Reform Bill a year later and he never sat for another. In 1833 he visited Egypt and the Holy Land on a tour of monastic libraries and rescued many valuable manuscripts. In 1841 he was appointed attaché at the Embassy at Constantinople. He later travelled in Italy in search of manuscripts and published *An Account of the Most Celebrated Libraries of Italy* in 1854.

Curzon was not content to accumulate; his primary aim was to illustrate a history of the art of writing from manuscripts in his own possession. The book which he contemplated was never finished, but his collection was deposited by his son in the British Museum. He was a pioneer in the quest for manuscripts little valued by their owners, but his successors soon found that their interest made the owners reluctant to sell. The chief object of his quest was to discover lost Greek or Roman classics, but the libraries had been so thoroughly explored in the fifteenth century by scholars with the same object in view that he found few Greek or Latin manuscripts older than those already in the British Museum. His most important discoveries were manuscripts in oriental languages.

An unexpected friendship sprang up between Curzon and Sir Thomas Phillipps, who compiled a list of Curzon's acquisitions. We have seen that Phillipps was a quarrelsome man, but this shared interest in the acquisition of manuscripts attracted him to Curzon. His domineering habits led him to offer his daughter's hand in marriage to the aristocratic Curzon without any indication from Curzon or, so far as we know, from his daughter that such a marriage would be welcome. Curzon had to write in some embarrassment to explain that the honour was not one that he sought.

Henry Huth (1815–78) was the son of a German merchant banker who came to England in 1809 and was naturalized. Henry Huth entered his father's business in 1833 but found it distasteful. He spent many years travelling on the Continent and in the United States and rejoined his father's firm in 1849. As a collector he ranged widely, collecting travel books, Elizabethan literature and early Spanish and German works, and collated every book himself. He was fastidious about condition.

Frederick Locker-Lampson (1821–95) in 1837 became a junior clerk in a colonial broker's office in London's Mincing Lane and did not like it. In 1841 he became a temporary clerk in Somerset House and in 1842 he was transferred to the Admiralty. His health broke down in 1849 and in 1850 he married a daughter of the seventh Earl of Elgin, who had brought the Elgin marbles to England. Soon afterwards he left government service. In 1857 he published his *London Lyrics* and in 1867 the anthology *Lyra Elegantiarum*, a collection of *vers de société*. His wife died in 1872 and in 1874 he married the only daughter of Sir Curtis Miranda Lampson of Rowfant, Sussex. In 1885 he took the name of Lampson. His *Rowfant Library* (1886) is a catalogue of his book-collection.

John Pierpont Morgan (1837–1913) has often been compared with Lorenzo the Magnificent because of the magnitude of his activities, financial and artistic. He was perhaps best known as a collector of works of art, but he also built up one of the world's great collections of rare books. His grandfather, Joseph, laid the foundations of the family fortunes in hotels and fire insurance. His father, Junius, was an international banker. The beginning of the Pierpont Morgan Collection was the gift by his father of the manuscript of *Guy Mannering* in the 1880s. Morgan was able to build up an outstanding collection within a single lifetime because he bought collections as well as books. In 1899 he bought the collection of books and manuscripts of the English bookseller James

Toovey, and in 1900 he acquired the Theodore Irwin collection of books and manuscripts for $200,000. In the same year he acquired the manuscripts and early printed books of Richard Bennett, a Manchester collector. This collection consisted of seven hundred volumes, all of the first importance and including thirty-two Caxtons. In 1904 he bought the Lewis Burchard Collection of some four hundred medieval romances, both printed books and manuscripts, which greatly enhanced the Library's holdings in the field of French literature. Morgan had a weakness for Caxtons and the Library has sixty-two of them in fine condition. Perhaps the most famous is the 1485 *Le Morte d'Arthur* which he bought for $42,800 at the Hoe sale in 1911–12 in competition with Huntington. Thereafter, continued competition between Morgan and Huntington did much to send up the prices of outstanding books and manuscripts.

In 1900 Morgan had a library built modelled on an Italian Renaissance palace. Miss Belle da Costa Greene was librarian for 43 years until her retirement in 1948. After the death of Pierpont Morgan in 1913, his son J. P. Morgan (1867–1943), together with Miss Greene, continued to build up the Library, which in 1924 was transferred to a board of trustees with an endowment of $1,500,000 for its maintenance.

Exhibitions had already made known the importance of the various collections which the Library comprised. In 1906 there was an exhibition at the Columbia University Library of some forty illuminated manuscripts and, after the Library had become public, there was an exhibition in 1924 in the New York Public Library of original manuscripts and drawings of English authors. The drawings included illustrations to the novels of Dickens by Cruikshank and Phiz and Du Maurier's pen sketches of *Trilby*. The manuscripts included those of R. L. Stevenson's *Strange Case of Dr Jekyll and Mr Hyde*, George Meredith's *Diana of the Crossways*, and ten novels of Sir Walter Scott. In the 1930 report on the Library the director claimed that the Library's most valuable contribution to American scholarship was the assembling of more than 750 illuminated or textual manuscripts dating from the sixth to the sixteenth century. Since then there have been further additions, including the *Blickling Homilies*, one of the most important Anglo-Saxon manuscripts. This was sold at auction in 1932 by order of the Marquis of Lothian for $55,000. The Library now contains over a thousand early manuscripts and over two thousand incunabula.

Almost every great public library owes an enormous amount to private collectors for building up collections which they passed to libraries at a fraction of their value. They help in other ways too. When the Luttrell Psalter, which had been displayed on loan in the British Museum for more than thirty years, was offered for sale in 1928, Pierpont Morgan not only abstained from bidding against the Museum, but lent them £64,830 free of interest for a year to enable them to buy the manuscript.

Henry Edwards Huntington (1850–1927) made his fortune by investing in railways and real estate in the western United States. When he retired at the age of sixty he was comparatively unknown to the world of books and was described as having 'a collection of some 30,000 not particularly distinguished volumes', but he then set to work to build up an outstanding collection of books, manuscripts and pictures. His two chief interests were English literature and Americana. His manuscripts included the original manuscript of Benjamin Franklin's *Autobiography*; his pictures included Gainsborough's *Blue Boy*. He bought the cream of the Rowfant Collection brought together by Frederick Locker-Lampson and from the Duke of Devonshire's library at Chatsworth he acquired twenty-five Caxtons, fifty-seven quartos of Shakespeare, a manuscript of the *Chester Mystery Plays*, and the outstanding collection of plays and playbills which the sixth Duke had bought from the actor John Philip Kemble. In 1917 he bought the Bridgewater House Library, which was particularly strong in works of the English Renaissance and which included the Ellesmere Chaucer, the best-known manuscript of the *Canterbury Tales*. The Huntington Library is now exceptionally strong in English literature before 1641. At first Huntington had shown little interest in incunabula, but from about 1916 he turned his attention to this expensive field and, by 1937, when a catalogue was published, the Library had acquired 5,291 separate titles, of which 126 are possibly unique.

Huntington began by buying rare and important books. He then turned his attention to background materials: little-known works on theology, science and everyday life, which acquired importance by being assembled in quantity. Finally he bought the modern reference books which research workers need to consult when working on older material. Although it has areas of special strength, the Library is not confined to any one period; it includes a well-balanced collection of first editions of English authors from Chaucer to Conrad. This balance has been achieved in part by the sale of duplicates from the collections which Huntington purchased *en bloc*. In a series of sales beginning in 1916 Huntington raised more than half a million dollars by the sale of duplicates. The building of the Library to house the collection at San Marino in California did something to redress the bibliophilic balance between the west and east coasts of the United States, which had previously been overwhelmingly weighted in favour of the east.

The collection of Henry Clay Folger (1857–1930) has aroused hostile comment among collectors and scholars for two reasons. The first is that he carried the accumulation of duplicates to a point much further than that reached by any other collector of rare books. The second is that at first he made no attempt to make his acquisitions available to scholars or to make use of them himself; once bought, they went straight into a bank vault. Folger's wholesale methods have greatly increased the rarity, and therefore the cost, of many works. About two hundred copies of the First Folio of Shakespeare are known to exist and of these the Folger

Library possesses seventy-nine. There is similar duplication of the other folios; of the four folios the Folger Library has about two hundred copies. The people most likely to resent this habit of 'bloating' are the collectors in the same field who find the books that they want unaccountably out of stock at their booksellers. Scholars find the practice easier to forgive because what Falconer Madan called 'the duplicity of duplicates' is now well known, and it is convenient to have a number of apparent duplicates together in the same library so that collation can reveal textual variants. The reproach of the bank vault has been removed because the collection is now housed in a library open to the public, close to the Library of Congress in Washington, thus solving one of the problems faced by founders of libraries of how to provide a large library of supporting material required by scholars when consulting a collection of rare books. The Library regards it as one of its chief responsibilities to make facsimiles available to scholars who work elsewhere.

In 1907 Folger bought from Marsden J. Perry the Shakespearean collection that had been built up by J. O. Halliwell-Phillipps and he also bought the collection of Lord Warwick. As we have seen, Folger was not blind to the appeal of the four folios of Shakespeare, but he realized that some of the quartos were much more rare. He secured the unique 1594 quarto of *Titus Andronicus* by sending an agent to its Swedish owner with an order for £2,000 in his pocket, thus outwitting two London booksellers who offered the same amount without having the money available for a cash transaction. In 1919 at the sale of part of the Britwell Court Library Folger was the under-bidder for a volume containing the fifth edition of *Venus and Adonis* (1599), which was sold to Huntington for $75,000. News of this sale caused the owners of old books to examine them carefully, and two small boys practising archery at Longner Hall, the property of Richard Francis Burton, were found to be using as target an old book fixed in a tree. The book proved to be a similar collection and it was sold to Folger for about $50,000. (In general Folger and

Huntington got on well with each other and avoided undue competition.)

The Folger Library is very strong in background material for the study of Shakespeare, including related manuscripts and critical studies and over a quarter of a million playbills. Since Folger's death in 1930 the most important addition to the Library was the purchase in 1938 of a collection of about 9,000 volumes from Sir Leicester Harmsworth, another large-scale collector in the Elizabethan field. Nearly a thousand items acquired from Harmsworth were unique.

The name of Michael Sadleir is so closely associated with nineteenth-century fiction that we tend to forget that he had many other bibliographical interests. In the preface to his *XIX Century Fiction: A Bibliographical Record* (CUP, 1951, 2 vols), he describes his interest as a collector in French literature of the Symbolist and Decadent schools, books about London, books printed on coloured paper and nineteenth-century private press publications. He was attracted to Trollope because his novels were cheap; it is largely a result of Sadleir's writings that they are so no longer. The choice of Trollope as the subject of a collection may seem to have been an easy one, but the challenge was presented by Sadleir's insistence that all his books should be in the finest possible condition. The surviving first editions of most of Trollope's novels are fairly plentiful, but they are very hard to find in good condition; they tend to be ex-library copies that have been read many times. One Victorian novelist led to another. Anthony Trollope's mother Frances and his brother Thomas Adolphus were both prolific novelists and Sadleir collected their works and then turned his attention to Marryat, Disraeli, Wilkie Collins and Mrs Gaskell. His choice of field illustrates the importance of timing to a collector. When Sadleir began to collect, Victorian novels had little appeal for collectors and they were cheap. He claimed that he never undertook the intensive collection of any author without the intention of ultimately writing a book – biography, bibliography or novel – about the author collected. His *Trollope: A Commentary*, a most readable book, was published in 1927 and his bibliography of Trollope's works appeared in the following year.

The novels which particularly attracted Sadleir were the 'Tales of Terror' or 'Gothic Romances' which flourished in England between 1770 and 1820. They have their counterparts in the crime fiction of today, but modern readers know about them chiefly from references in novels of more permanent value. Catherine Morland in Jane Austen's *Northanger Abbey* found it hard to tear herself away from them. In collecting the Gothic Romances Sadleir learnt the difference between an expensive book and a scarce one. Some of the novels are by well-known authors, and these are expensive but easy to find. The really difficult items are those that no one has ever heard of but which, when found, can be bought cheaply unless the collector has put up the price against himself by the assiduity of his search.

Sadleir showed skill in his choice of fields. Tales of Terror and Victorian novels were both rare and unwanted. When they did turn up they were often in large collections which Sadleir bought *en bloc*. In 1938 he parted with his entire collection of Gothic Novels except for a few duplicates. He was attracted by unfashionable books and his large-scale book-buying made them fashionable. He deliberately avoided the works of major novelists like Scott and Dickens on the grounds that they were well-known to both bibliographers and booksellers, and a complete collection in the condition that he aimed at would have been beyond his means. He also avoided novels published in parts. He was a publisher as well as a collector and an author, and his knowledge of publishing was of value to him as a bibliographer. In his *The Evolution of Publishers' Binding Styles 1770–1900* (Constable 1930) he showed himself to be a pioneer in one aspect of bibliography that had been virtually ignored.

Perhaps the most famous author collection in the world is the Horace Walpole Collection of Wilmarth Lewis at Farmington, Connecticut. Its importance is due partly to its owner's enthusiasm and drive in overcoming obstacles and partly to the harmony of tastes between collector and subject. Lewis, like Walpole, was attracted by relics as well as by the books and manuscripts of which most author collections consist. Horace Walpole wrote in 1756:

> You would laugh if you saw in the midst of what trumpery I am writing. Two porters have just brought home my purchases: . . . old broken pots, pans, and pipkins, a lantern of scraped oyster-shells, scimitars, Turkish pipes, Chinese baskets, etc., etc., . . . P.S. I forgot that I was outbid for Oliver Cromwell's nightcap.[1]

Lewis notes that all these things and the other contents of Strawberry Hill have now become relics. He says, with regret, 'I have, I am sorry to say, no wisp of Horace Walpole's hair.'[2] Walpole left an unusually large and varied accumulation of relics – prints, pictures, enamels, coins, china and furniture – to provide scope for a future collector with Lewis's energy and enthusiasm.

Walpole is best known as a letter-writer, and the chief interest of Wilmarth Lewis's collection is in the letters. He realized that it is not only the letters written by an eminent man that are worth collecting; those written to him may be full of interest and are sometimes necessary to explain allusions in the eminent man's own letters. About seven thousand letters to and from Walpole are believed to be in existence. Lewis reported in 1952 that he then had the originals of 2,600 of these and photostats of 2,500 more, and it may be assumed that the numbers are now larger. The printed books in the collection include all the editions of Walpole's works, with

[1] Wilmarth Lewis, *Collector's Progress*, pp. 135 f.
[2] loc. cit.

some manuscripts, about eight hundred and fifty books from Walpole's library and the productions of his private press at Strawberry Hill. An author collection extends indefinitely from a nucleus of the author's works, and Lewis's collection includes ten thousand eighteenth-century letters besides those to and from Walpole.

The collection forms the basis of the massive *Yale Edition of Horace Walpole's Correspondence*, begun in 1933 and planned to fill fifty volumes. Part of the background material for this edition is a 'diurnal', recording what is known of Walpole on every day of his life from his twentieth year to his eightieth. Lewis planned an even more ambitious extension of his collection when he tried to acquire every book printed in Britain between 1751 and 1800 that is not in the Yale University Library. He later modified this plan, excluding subjects like theology, verse and fiction that are already well represented at Yale. The subjects excluded are considerable but those that remain include a large number of miscellaneous books, each one unimportant in itself but together providing splendid material for the study of day-to-day life in the eighteenth century. Another large-scale project of Lewis's was an experiment in inter-library co-operation known as the Farmington Plan. In 1942 a group of collectors and librarians met under his chairmanship to discuss how the great research libraries might divide up the field of human knowledge, each library being responsible for one subject, to ensure that there should be at least two copies of every foreign printed book somewhere in the United States available for inter-library loans. Lewis announced his intention that his collection should ultimately form part of the Yale University Library and, when this became known, university librarians showed generosity in allowing him to acquire, by purchase or exchange, books in their possession that had once belonged to Walpole. Lewis's thoroughness, his decision that his collection should be kept together after his death and his ambitious project of publishing Walpole's letters have assured that he will rank as one of the world's great collectors, not merely because of the quantity of material that he accumulated but because of the good use that he made of it.

Some libraries grow slowly, but Lord Rothschild's collection of English books of the eighteenth century was built up in a period of twelve years from 1936 to 1948. The collection, the catalogue of which runs to eight hundred pages, illustrates the splendid results that can follow from the application of university disciplinary procedures. When Lord Rothschild was an undergraduate at Cambridge in 1932 he was obliged to spend a year working for an Ordinary Degree. One of his subjects was English Literature, and George Rylands of King's College encouraged him to buy eighteenth-century books, beginning with an edition of Addison needed for his course. One of the books that he bought at this time is still in the Rothschild Collection; the others, the collector reports with admirable modesty in the catalogue of his collection, 'were books of the sort which bibliophiles often buy at the beginning of their collecting career'.

The Rothschild Library, like Michael Sadleir's collection, is a good example of the importance of skilful timing and choice of a field in the building up of a collection. If Lord Rothschild had chosen an earlier century, there would not have been enough material available even for a collector of his very considerable means. He was able to take advantage of the reaction against the eighteenth century which followed the boom of the 1920s. The collection is especially strong in the works of Swift, including 315 books or manuscripts by him as well as a large collection of Swiftiana and books from Swift's library.

Beside the works by eighteenth-century authors which form the bulk of the collection, there are collections of the publications of the Baskerville, Foulis and Strawberry Hill Presses and a collection of bindings. Like most great collections, the Rothschild Library owes something to earlier collections which it absorbed *en masse*. These include the plays collected by Lord Rolle of Stevenstone (1750–1842), whose library was dispersed in 1946. An excellent catalogue of the collection was privately printed at the Cambridge University Press in two volumes in 1954, and this serves as a useful guide for anyone who wishes to specialize in the eighteenth century.

CHAPTER VII

BOOKSELLERS

IT is by now well known that writing books, though a
pleasant hobby, is not as a rule a good way of making a
living. Recent trends suggest that the same remark could
be made with equal truth about selling them. The problem of
inducing people to buy books has been eloquently set forth
by Felix Dahn:

> To write a book is a task needing only pen, ink and paper; to
> print a book is rather more difficult, because genius often
> expresses itself illegibly; to read a book is more difficult still, for
> one has to struggle with sleep; but to sell a book is the most
> difficult task of all.[1]

Writers, unless they are authors of best-sellers, are wise to
secure for themselves another source of income, and booksellers are tending to follow their example. Dealers in new
books combine that activity with selling stationery or gramo-
phone records, and dealers in second-hand books are showing
an increasing fondness for carrying on their business from a
private address and advertising that their business is by post or
appointment only. For the bookseller the practice has the
advantage that it requires very little capital; for the customer
it has the disadvantage that he has fewer opportunities to
browse, and the modern equivalent of the fourpenny box is
no longer there to encourage the impecunious student in the
habit of book-buying and to allow the bookseller to get rid of
his junk.

[1] *Frank Arthur Mumby, Publishing and Bookselling,* rev. edn. (Jonathan Cape
1949), p. 329.

The problem of what is a reasonable margin of profit is comparatively easy for the dealer in new books, because it is largely out of his own control. Dr Johnson wrote to Dr Nathan Wetherell, Master of University College, Oxford, about the terms on which the University Press should issue books. Johnson suggested that a wholesaler should get ten per cent and a country bookseller, selling a book published at twenty shillings, should get three and sixpence profit. Using language that would be just as applicable today, Johnson says: 'With less profit than this . . . the country bookseller cannot live; for his receipts are small and his debts sometimes bad.'[1]

In the late nineteenth century discounts from booksellers to customers began at ten per cent and gradually increased to twenty-five per cent. On 1 January 1900 British publishers established the net book agreement to prevent the sale of new books at reduced prices except in special conditions.

A second-hand bookseller's survival in business depends upon his judgement in deciding how much he is willing to pay for the books he buys and what prices he can reasonably charge for those that he sells. In answering these questions his best guide is his own experience of buying and selling reinforced by the information that he can gain about the experience of other booksellers. He learns his job partly by studying the catalogues of other booksellers.

One dealer in second-hand furniture acquired a library along with the rest of the contents of a house and found the task of pricing the books too difficult. He finally offered them in three categories: large books a shilling, medium-sized books ninepence, and small books sixpence. His approach was unsound as well as lacking in subtlety, for any book-collector knows the large books have a better chance of survival than pamphlets and are therefore likely, other things being equal, to be cheaper.

There are two simple factors which are often forgotten by those who talk about book prices. The first is the difference

---

[1] Boswell's *Life of Johnson*, ed. George Birkbeck Hill (OUP), II, 426.

between a bookseller's buying price and his selling price. One sometimes feels that a typical second-hand bookshop is controlled by two partners: a pessimist on prices who looks after the buying and an optimist who marks the selling price. There can be no exact and constant relation between these two prices. Much will depend on the value of the book; a bookseller is entitled to a higher percentage of profit on a cheap book because some of his expenses are the same whatever the price of the book. We all admit theoretically that a bookseller must live, but when we are considering how much he ought to pay for books we tend to assume that a bookseller who makes a profit is cheating the customer. In fact a second-hand bookseller will not remain in business long unless he makes a very large percentage of profit on cheap books.

Another factor that should determine the profit margin is the length of time that the bookseller expects to have to stock the book. Booksellers, like other merchants, have to decide whether to adopt a policy of small profit with quick returns or of keeping a book in stock for a long time and selling it eventually at a high price. Another factor is bulk. Many years ago I paid £8 for the Cook-Wedderburn edition of Ruskin, which now costs several hundred pounds, because a bookseller felt that he needed the shelf-space that the thirty-nine bulky volumes took up.

The other economic factor that is often overlooked in the discussion of the prices of really old books is the rate at which money accumulates at compound interest over a long period. An Elizabethan quarto may have cost sixpence when published and several hundred pounds today, but it will generally be found that the increase in value has not kept pace with the rate at which an investment of money would have appreciated.

A low-priced book is not necessarily a cheap one. Cheap books are those that are acquired by some accident at less than their current value. Prices can vary very much from one century to the next. Narcissus Luttrell (1657–1732) was able to buy flimsy volumes, now worth hundreds of pounds, for prices from a penny to sixpence. At that time book-buyers wanted more solid volumes.

A book may be obviously desirable without reaching a high price so long as it remains in print, because potential purchasers think that there is no hurry to buy, but as soon as it goes out of print the price is liable to shoot up. If there is no demand for a book, its degree of rarity is irrelevant. When we consider demand we are concerned not only with the number but also with the wealth of potential purchasers, and this fact introduces into the question of price an element of accident dependent upon fashion. Two factors which affect price in so far as they may affect demand are the intrinsic importance of the book and the condition of the copy offered.

Book auction records give a rough indication of value, but they give only the vaguest indication of condition, and many accidental factors may make a single auction price unreliable: the presence or absence of a wealthy specialist collector or, more important still, of two wealthy collectors, or the possibility that two bidders may be tempted in their enthusiasm to make silly bids. Sales of important collections make higher prices even for the minor books than miscellaneous sales. The presence at the sale of a number of booksellers with capital behind them may exercise a steadying influence, their experience preventing prices from going too high and their capital enabling them to take a long view and so prevent prices from going too low.

Some isolated transactions can clearly be an excellent investment. In a time of rising prices, prices do not rise uniformly, and it is possible in most bookshops to find little pockets of forgotten books still marked at the prices that were current twenty or thirty years ago. If they belong to a category that has in the meantime come into fashion, they may be worth twenty times their marked prices. Volumes of seventeenth-century sermons could be bought at £1 for a volume of a dozen or more sermons before the publication of D. G. Wing's *Short-title Catalogue of Books printed in England, Scotland, Ireland, Wales and British America and of English*

Books printed in other Countries 1641–1700 (New York, 1945–51, 3 vols.). But now each item has a separate Wing number and such a volume might easily sell for more than £30. These occasional finds are more than counterbalanced by the numerous occasions when a bookseller says that he generally sells such volumes for a few shillings but for some reason he does not seem to have any in stock at the moment. The customer could tell him the reason: he is selling them too cheaply. But it would be the height of folly to regard such discoveries as typical. It would be much more true to assume that, with a few exceptions, a book fetches its highest price when it is new, that it sinks in value rather quickly when it reaches the second-hand bookshop and that it then continues to sink slowly in price until it reaches its value as waste-paper.

Some booksellers claim that they pass on bargains to their customers by adding a fixed percentage to the buying price. The temptation to depart from such a policy must be great, and no bookseller should be expected to carry it out. Why should he receive no reward for the knowledge and experience which enable him to recognize a bargain? Every time that he buys a book he takes a chance on ever selling it again, and he needs a large percentage of profit on some books to make up for the large number of books that he has to write off as a total loss. Book-collectors are liable to quote the prices at which they have seen a second-hand book advertised without asking for evidence that it has ever been sold at that price.

Rosenbach was an unashamed advocate of charging whatever price the market would bear. The Boston physician, Dr Harvey Cushing, returned a book to him because he was unwilling to pay four times what it had cost at a public sale. Rosenbach's reply was uncompromising: 'I do not consider four hundred per cent a large profit, or ten thousand per cent large. We place a price on the volume based on what we consider its worth, regardless of its cost. Customers evidently agree with us.'[1]

---

[1] Edwin Wolf and John F. Fleming, op. cit., p. 236.

The acquisition of valuable books from aristocratic owners who have little interest in them and who need the money is a delicate operation. The vendors are liable to be particularly sensitive because they have a feeling of guilt in parting with family possessions. Rosenbach failed to buy the Boswell papers at Malahide Castle. In 1925 he sent a telegram to Lord Talbot saying that he would be interested in acquiring them and received a chilling reply signed by Joyce Talbot de Malahide: 'We regret that such Boswell papers as are in our possession are neither for sale, nor can be seen by anyone. Lord Talbot was very surprised and annoyed at the matter being opened by telegram.'[1]

What the book-buyer would like is a valuation like that of shares on the stock exchange, quoting both a dealer's buying price and his selling price. In times of uncertainty or for books in little demand, the price will be 'wide'; for rarities in great demand it will be 'narrow'. Such an approach would be appropriate for expensive books.

A mark of the successful bookseller is the ability to notice the significant detail that may increase the value of a book a hundredfold. One of Rosenbach's greatest achievements was the purchase for £57 of Philip Pain's *Daily Meditations*, or *Quotidian Preparations for and Considerations of Death and Eternity*, printed at Cambridge by Marmaduke Johnson in 1668. The author seems to have gone out of his way to make the book seem uninteresting, and after the sale several people, including the auctioneer, asked Rosenbach why he had paid £57 for a dull theological poem worth only a few shillings. Rosenbach had realized that the place of publication was not Cambridge, England but Cambridge, Massachusetts and that Marmaduke Johnson was the printer of the famous Eliot Indian Bible. He had thus bought the only known copy of the first volume of verse printed in North America. When the auctioneer asked how much he would have paid for the book, Rosenbach replied, 'Oh, £8,000 or £9,000.'

[1] op. cit., p. 224

A collector must expect to pay more for a book which is reported to him than for one which he digs out, because he must pay for the bookseller's time and trouble. It is true that a bookseller reporting on a book does not have the expense of keeping it in stock for a long time, but the bookseller who reports needs his commission in addition to the profit of the bookseller in whose shop he finds the book. Some small booksellers, often a book lover whose only premises are the house in which he lives, specialize in looking for specified books and have very little stock.

Books are not always dearer in capital cities than in the provinces. A provincial bookseller who acquires a book known to be in demand sometimes gets excited and prices it too high, whereas the bookseller in London's West End, who has sold many rarer books, is more restrained.

There is a lot to be said for adopting the rule: 'When in doubt, buy.' For one thing the market in rare books, as in other collectable objects, is steadily rising, so that it is quite likely that the next copy that you see will be dearer. It is quite possible that another copy will come along at a slightly lower price, but, as Lord Keynes said, 'In the long run we are all dead.' It's no good if the other copy comes along after the buyer's collecting life is over. No important collection has been built up unless the collector was willing to pay more for some items than they were worth.

The books that are collected form a very small proportion of those that are published. Fashions in collecting can play havoc with any general rule about prices, but, if a book makes any lasting appeal to collectors, it can be assumed that it will rise in price over a long period and it may take a swift leap forward as the result of a change in fashion.

Auction sales are among the sources of information that help a bookseller to learn his job. Many of the booksellers present at auction sales have no intention of buying; they are simply studying the market. An inexperienced buyer faces many dangers, chief of which is the 'ring' of booksellers, which in its simplest form in now illegal. Two or three dealers bid on behalf of the ring and after the sale the members of the group hold a second auction among themselves, known as the 'knock-out'. At the second sale prices are higher and the extra money made is shared out among the participants. A function of the ring is to prevent outsiders from securing bargains and to leave them to purchase lots pushed up to inflated prices. Any loss involved is shared among the members of the ring. Booksellers can afford to force prices up against the private bidder because, if left with a book at an unduly high price, they can spread their loss among their other purchases. If a private buyer wants to bid, he is wise to give his bid to the auctioneer before the sale or to pay a bookseller his ten per cent commission to bid for him. A bookseller may reasonably refuse to accept a commission if the limit is too low, because he may himself be a competitor and it is hard on him if he has to buy a book for his customer if it goes for a bargain price but for himself if it doesn't. A bookseller who bought a book for me at £40 said that he would have been willing to pay much more than that to buy it for his own stock. His commission was an inadequate reward for his forbearance. A bookseller who acts as agent accepts responsibility for inspecting the book to see that it is free from faults and for advising on the bid necessary to secure it.

In advertisements of country house sales the standard of cataloguing is sometimes very low. One such advertisement contained many references to an author called Rutkin but the mystery of his identity was solved by the inclusion among the books offered of Volume III of *Modern Painters*. Odd volumes had obviously been picked out at random. Such an advertisement might attract bidders who would conclude from the quality of the cataloguing that the auctioneers knew nothing about books. The best bargains are likely to be found at sales and in shops where books are an inconsiderable proportion of the goods offered for sale.

In the nineteenth century book-auctions were regarded as wholesale operations, and many booksellers would like to keep them that way today. Auctioneers like to deal with booksellers because they know which of them are worthy of credit and, when they sell to experts, there is a better chance that faults will be detected before rather than after a sale. Moreover, a preponderance of booksellers among the bidders gives stability to prices. A wildly high bid brings short-term gains to the auctioneer, but in the long run it is bad for the book business as a whole. Nobody in the book trade wants the idea to get about that prices are erratic.

Many collectors pick up bargains from one bookseller in order to sell them at a profit to another. It is sometimes said that the proper thing to do is to tell the bookseller that the book is underpriced. I do not accept this view. In the first place we cannot assume that the bookseller would welcome such gratuitous advice. One bookseller, normally a most kindly man, replied to a customer who protested that the bookseller was letting him have a book too cheaply: 'Please allow me to know my own business. I didn't pay anything for it.'

Those who think that customers have a duty to point out to a bookseller that his prices are too low should remember that the bookseller has bought the book at a price based upon his own estimate of its worth, not upon that which the customer's special knowledge would cause him to give it. Virtually all second-hand booksellers base their prices on their estimate of what the market will bear, not on the prices that they have paid. If a customer insists on paying a bookseller £100 for a book marked at £10, is there any serious likelihood that the bookseller will pass it on to the man from whom he bought it? If a book turns out to be worth very much more than the bookseller paid for it, it is reasonable that the unexpected profit should go to the man who has the knowledge, often dearly bought, that will enable him to recognize the book's value. That man will usually be the bookseller but, if it happens to be a customer, there is no reason why he should make the bookseller a present of his knowledge.

Percy Muir records that, when he was a partner in the firm of Elkin Mathews, an American bookseller was charged prices much higher than those marked in the catalogue that was then at press. He says that 'the disclosure of such *faux pas* was the cause of a good laugh all round'. Not quite all round for he adds: 'clients did not always react so light-heartedly.'[1]

To set against such incidents many of us can recall instances of outstanding honesty and generosity on the part of book-sellers. I have myself many times profited from the kindness of Joseph David Hughes, who opened a shop in Manchester in partnership with John Sherratt in 1896, and I was the more pleased to read an anecdote which shows an honest bookseller at his best:

> The story goes that an elderly lady, obviously undernourished, called there one day with two first editions of Shelley's poems, and asked a modest £1 for the pair. Hughes sent her to a nearby café, with two shillings to buy sustenance, while he valued the books. When she returned to the shop he told her they were worth £450, and she fainted. Brandy was ordered, and when she recovered, the booksellers explained that they had not sufficient capital to make her an outright offer, but, instead, proposed paying her 30s. per week until the amount was paid off. The lady accepted – and brandy was always kept on the premises thereafter.[2]

It is not without regret that, as a book-buyer, I say that booksellers know their job, and it is not often that they need advice from customers to raise their prices. The converse situation is more common. What is a book-buyer to do if he sees a book marked at a price that seems to him to be too high? If the bookseller is a stranger, the book-buyer must do as he did when the book was too cheap: accept the situation and either pay the exorbitant price or do without the book.

Some collectors estrange booksellers by a love of haggling.

---

[1] Percy H. Muir, *Minding My Own Business* (Chatto, 1956), p. 58.
[2] Frank Arthur Mumby and Ian Norrie, *Publishing and Bookselling*, 5th edn., (Jonathan Cape, 1974), pp. 295 f.

If a collector is too ready to haggle, he will find that a book-seller will not sell a rarity to him if he can find another buyer. On the other hand Scott's Jonathan Oldbuck gives one reason for haggling: 'How often have I stood haggling on a half-penny lest, by a too ready acquiescence in the dealer's first price, he should be led to suspect the value I set upon the article!' (*The Antiquary*, chapter 3). Collectors soon learn that it is wise not to seem too eager to acquire a book, and there is a good biblical description of a collector who adopts this policy: 'It is naught, it is naught, saith the buyer, but when he is gone his way, then he boasteth' (*Proverbs* xx. 14). Some eminent collectors have been notorious hagglers. The book-seller may enter into the spirit of the thing and extol his wares with emotion. Rosenbach used to do this and by his behaviour caused one customer to say: 'All right, don't cry, Dr Rosen-bach, I'm going to buy it.'

When the bookseller and the customer get to know each other well, however, the position is different, and haggling may be an advantage to both parties. The reason why a book-seller finds a stranger's haggling so offensive is that it suggests that the bookseller doesn't know his job. No second-hand bookseller could remain in business unless he knew more about the values of books than most of his customers, but the bookseller is a general practitioner and the customer may be a specialist. There is usually a small field in which the customer knows more about prices than the bookseller does. When the bookseller and the customer know each other well, the book-seller may profit by the customer's specialized knowledge, partly because by then he knows what is the customer's special field and partly because he can trust the customer not to mislead him.

Booksellers need to arrive at a quick decision about the rarity of the books they handle. There are many degrees of rarity. The term 'collectors' item' is sometimes used to describe a book which, by its condition or rarity, can be ex-pected to make a strong appeal to collectors. One bookseller coined the term 'burglar's item' to denote a book so rare that the only way of obtaining a copy is to burgle one of the national libraries. There is a further degree of rarity, consisting of books which are known to have existed but of which not a single copy has survived. Sometimes fragments of these lost books survive, single leaves or parts of leaves incorporated in the binding of other books.

Rarity alone is not enough to make a book valuable. The position was summed up by one bookseller who agreed with a customer: 'Yes, that book is rare, but nothing like so rare as people who want to buy it.' A bookseller cannot decide in a vacuum that a book has an absolute value; he has to pay attention to his stock and his customers. A bookseller once refused to buy a rather handsome book that was offered to him at a low price. His reply was, 'Yes, it's a very nice book, and I shall be very glad to buy it – when I've sold the two copies I already have.'

Estimates of rarity are largely a subjective matter. 'There were only a certain number of them printed' did not inspire confidence when applied by a bookseller's assistant to a six-penny picture-book published by the Victoria & Albert Museum. In one sense it is true of any book; if it was intended to suggest that the book was rare, it was a lie.

In the advertising of all collectable objects a process of inflation occurs. A coin offered 'in good condition' by a trustworthy dealer might seem to be attractive, but the term has been applied with excessive optimism so often that it is almost an insult to a coin to describe it in this way. 'Good' was replaced by 'fine' and this in its turn came to be applied to coins that were not really in a condition that made them attractive to collectors. This meant that 'fine' had to be reinforced by an adverb, and now few collectors would be interested in a coin that was not at least in 'very fine' (VF) condition and he would prefer it to be 'extremely fine' (EF). Once these conventions have become established, they are observed with fidelity by reputable dealers, but a customer has to begin by learning the language of the trade and to learn which dealers can be trusted to use it with care. Bookselling has its own conventions, but they are not observed so rigorously or so uniformly as those of coin dealers. A book may be described as 'excessively rare' or in 'extremely good' condition, but it is necessary to know what meaning the bookseller attaches to these terms. Until such knowledge is acquired, it is well to ask for each item on approval, even if the bookseller advertises that he gives preference to firm orders.

Rarity has always to be considered in relation to demand. The First Folio of Shakespeare is not really scarce, since between two hundred and three hundred copies still exist. It is expensive because of the demand. Some books are rare because they were published in very small editions. An author may have a set of uncorrected page-proofs bound up and distributed to friends. Some publishers prepare such copies for distribution to booksellers or critics as part of the advance publicity. The question that arises is how far such an issue may be said ever to have been genuinely published. Sometimes a pamphlet may bear on its title-page the words 'Printed for private circulation'. Many of Tennyson's early poems exist in very small editions of this kind, notably *The Lover's Tale* (1833), of which six copies were printed. One of these was sold in 1924 for £1,400. Many of Kipling's works can be found published in flimsy yellow-wrapped pamphlets, often containing a single short poem. These are editions issued by his American publishers to secure American copyright. Such flimsy pamphlets would normally have a poor chance of survival, but these were published after collectors had begun to realize the value of such ephemera, and the many collectors of Kipling see to it that they are not destroyed.

A book may be suppressed for many different reasons, especially if the author is rich enough to bear the cost. The author may be dissatisfied with the book production; he may have changed his mind on some points or fear that he may give offence; the book may contain a libel or it may have been printed without the authority of the owner of the copyright.

When it is known that a book is to be suppressed, the few copies that have been published become valuable, partly because readers suspect possible improprieties and partly because collectors know that limitation of supplies will send up the price.

The reason why Dickens's novels in parts are so expensive is that the parts were treated as magazines are today and destroyed in large numbers. A first edition of *Pickwick Papers* in parts is worth very much more than a first edition of *Edwin Drood* because the printing order of an author's early book is small and the chances of destruction greater.

Rarity results from demand in excess of supply. The reasons for a small supply are very varied: the author might be little known at the time of publication; fragility or unimpressive appearance of a book would increase its chances of destruction; absorption by libraries could lead to copies being 'read to bits' or reduced to a state which makes them not collectable.

The really high prices are fetched by the little-known works of authors who later became famous. Their later better-known works are less costly because they were published in larger editions. A pioneer work of any kind is also likely to fetch a high price. Such a book is *The Bay Psalm Book* (1640), because it is the oldest surviving book printed in North America, and books with an American interest have become very popular.

Any attempt to indicate degrees of rarity based upon the number of copies available must fail because a book is rare only in relation to demand. 'Rare' means that there are more buyers than sellers and 'very rare' means that there are many more. Rarity can vary from time to time with the varying reputations of authors. Books that have been popular may survive in bookshops when there is no longer any demand for them. In the early years of the present century reprints of the novels of Meredith and Bulwer Lytton could be bought for a few pence because they had once been popular but were so no longer.

A change of taste or a new discovery may stimulate interest in a class of books that has hitherto been little regarded. The available copies are quickly sold and prices rise. The rise may be only temporary because publicity given to high prices draws books out of their attics. The recent publicity given to the high prices paid for old photographs must have caused many people to examine the family album with a new interest. The books that are brought to the market in this way generally belong to the middle range: books that are too good to throw away but not good enough to remember until they begin to be mentioned in the news.

A new source of books may be opened up as a result of war or political upheaval. The incredible wealth of Sir Thomas Phillipps's collection of manuscripts was the result of the destruction of many monastic libraries during the Napoleonic Wars, and the two world wars of the present century brought on to the market many books which were previously regarded as rare and which have become rare again since the new supplies have been absorbed.

Some books are rare because they were made of ephemeral materials. Many eighteenth-century plays are printed on paper of poor quality and many nineteenth-century books are cheaply bound. Trollope's *The Duke's Children* (3 vols, 1880) was wire-stapled and therefore falls apart easily. Charlotte Brontë's *Shirley* (3 vols, 1849) was bound in a friable fabric and the result is that the joints split. Often the cloth fades easily, as in *In Memoriam* (1850) and *The Woman in White* (3 vols, 1860).[1]

An unjustified rumour that a book is rare may become self-fulfilling, because book-buyers who believe it withdraw copies from the market by buying them, and the copies that remain become in fact rare.

Booksellers sometimes make excessive use of the statement that a book is not in a particular bibliography, even when the so-called bibliography is the catalogue of a private collection.

[1] John Carter, *Taste and Technique in Book-Collecting*, p. 153.

The absence of a book from the *Short-Title Catalogue* may indicate rarity, but there are many other possible reasons. A book expressing unpopular opinions, politically or theologically, would not appear in the records of the Company of Stationers unless the author or printer was caught. Many books were not entered because of ignorance of the necessity for registration or fear of competition from other publishers. Some books were entered and never published, others entered under one title and published under another. A book may be omitted from *Book Auction Records* because it is so rare that no copy has been sold, but a much more common reason for its exclusion is that it is so common that when sold it forms part of a mixed lot.

Second-hand booksellers have often included eccentrics among their number and some of them seem to have a hatred of casual customers who come into their shops and interfere with their reading. A cartoon published in a booksellers' magazine showed a domineering woman in a second-hand bookshop asking if the bookseller had a copy of the poems of Browning. The bookseller replied hesitantly 'Er, no, madam' and received the crushing rebuke 'No, you wouldn't have'. The point of the drawing is that the bookseller is keeping out of sight a copy of Browning's poems that he was reading when the customer came in. It may be that the bookseller who hates his customers is suffering from conflicts of emotion when forced to sell books that he would much rather keep himself. Bookbuyers tolerate a lack of co-operation from booksellers as one of the hazards of the game of book-hunting, and sometimes it can be explained by the unwillingness of the public to buy books. If people will not buy books, it does not pay a bookseller to keep a good stock. Today the bookseller is liable to make a charge for packing as well as postage. In *The Daily Telegraph* for 27 August 1973 a reader wrote complaining that a university bookseller had threatened to close his account unless he undertook to spend at least £10 a year. In the short term one can see the bookseller's point of view, although the customer couldn't, but in the long term booksellers, like stockbrokers, would probably be wise to welcome small accounts in the hope that one day they may grow into big ones.

High postal charges are playing havoc with the book trade. At one time a customer could take it for granted that, if a book was not in stock, a bookseller would offer to get it for him. He can no longer make this assumption, because on an order for a single book postage and other expenses may well exceed the bookseller's margin of profit. At the same time it is a short-sighted policy for the bookseller to be uncooperative. The practice of ordering a book for a customer is one that has enabled small booksellers to survive. If it is abandoned, book-buyers will take their custom to larger bookshops which are more likely to have the required volume in stock. At today's prices to keep a large stock of books other than best-sellers demands a large investment of capital. A recent order for £100's worth of books from a large bookshop revealed that only £4's worth were in stock. If booksellers cannot afford either to stock or to order books, what is to become of the trade in new books? As a wayfarer was once expected to order a drink at a village pub 'for the good of the house', book-buyers may include among their reasons for buying a particular book that it may help to keep a useful bookseller in business. Booksellers, for their part, can co-operate by stocking a range of books wider than the list of textbooks and best-sellers on which many booksellers rely.

Book-buyers need an opportunity to see important new books on a wide range of subjects before deciding whether to buy them, and the capital needed by a bookseller to provide such a service is considerable. The root of the problem is that people do not buy enough books. If they did, booksellers would be more willing to invest the necessary capital and to take the risk of being left with a large stock of unsold expensive scholarly books. The expansion of universities has brought with it many difficulties, but it is to be hoped that this is one problem which expansion will help to solve.

Universities ought to provide enough purchasers of serious books to support a good bookshop, even if the proportion of non-starters among the public remains as high as it is at present. Universities can encourage booksellers to adopt a more adventurous policy by making sites available on favourable terms to booksellers who are willing to do more than skim the remunerative textbook trade, and orders of books for the university library could be used as an inducement to booksellers to stock unremunerative books and to encourage browsing.

The attempt of efficiency experts to impose order on a bookshop may be misguided. One large bookshop which has grown from a merging of several smaller shops, conducted a survey as a result of complaints that customers found it difficult to find their way about in it. One reply was: 'I *like* bookshops where I can't find my way around. I come in to browse and I like it vaguely chaotic and not like a supermarket.' In one bookshop a customer, trying to be helpful, arranged the books on display in neat piles but he was followed round by an assistant restoring the piles to their former haphazard state. The bookseller's point of view has been expressed by Arnold Bennett. In *Riceman Steps* (1923 Part II, Chapter 6) Henry Earlforward, a second-hand bookseller, finds that his wife has decided to give him a pleasant surprise by cleaning and tidying his shop:

'My dear, you're ruining my business,' he said mildly and blandly.

'Henry!' She stopped near the foot of the stairs, as it were thunderstruck by a revelation.

'You don't understand how much of it depends on me having lots of books lying about as if they weren't anything at all. That's just what book-collectors like. If everything was shipshape they wouldn't look twice at the place. Whenever they see a pile of books in the dark they think there must be bargains.'

A survey of the sales of a typical bookshop revealed that a

large proportion of the sales are not concerned with great literature but with the satisfaction of everyday practical needs for such things as guide books, textbooks, children's books and detective stories. It also revealed that the average cost of new books sold in a bookshop is quite low, though rising every day. In 1968 in one bookshop sixty-six per cent of the books sold cost under ten shillings.

Many booksellers stay in business by selling stationery and fancy goods. Others rely on the sale of books at a discount to libraries and schools, so they are naturally alarmed by cuts in budgets and by the action of some education authorities in exploring the possibilities of buying books direct from publishers.

CHAPTER VIII

FORGERIES

C OLLECTORS always have to be on their guard against books that are not what they seem to be, but it is not always proper to describe the offending volume as a forgery. There are many different kinds of deception. A collector once acquired a short unpublished manuscript of a famous author. He asked a printer to print three copies as a pamphlet and locked them away, thinking that he had the entire stock of a pamphlet of excessive rarity. He was disconcerted to find that a copy of his pamphlet had been sold at auction at a high price, although his three copies were still in his possession. Clearly the printer had disobeyed his instructions and printed one or more copies for himself. The printer's action was improper, but the copies kept by him can be claimed as perfectly genuine.

Facsimiles are on the fringes of forgery. If a leaf of a valuable book is missing, it can be replaced by a facsimile without any intention to deceive. The technique of reproduction is constantly improving and it is often difficult to distinguish a facsimile from the original. The paper is the most difficult to match but restorers of old books often have a large stock of paper taken from the fly-leaves of old books. This is no doubt the explanation for many of the books that are offered for sale 'with blank leaf at end missing'. The man who has supplied the missing leaf and the collector or bookseller who employs him may both make it clear that one leaf is a facsimile, but the book survives them both and it may afterwards be sold as perfect.

Paper covers are often missing from old pamphlets and

these are easily supplied or transferred from a less valuable book because they were often blank paper.

Bindings of famous collectors have often been forged. Many bindings supposed to have been created for Diane de Poitiers were made by a Belgian binder Louis Hagué for his dupe John Blacken in the 1890s. The books themselves were genuine.

There were often sound reasons for deception. In the Reformation period it was a common practice, both in England and on the Continent, to publish books with false imprints and dates much earlier than the real date of publication in order to mislead the civil and ecclestiastical authorities. In England the practice was especially common with Catholic publications, since the Catholics were a persecuted minority. The Jesuit Robert Parsons operated a secret press at various places in the provinces and printed five small tracts with title-pages stating that they had been printed at Douai by John Lyon.

Literary imposture is of many kinds, and all could be represented in a collection. In 1760 there was published at Edinburgh *Fragments of Ancient Poetry Collected in the Highlands of Scotland*. These were described as specimens of ancient Gaelic poetry collected by James Macpherson and they were said to be by an early Gaelic poet called Ossian. Dr Johnson always refused to accept Macpherson's claim that the Ossian poems were genuine translations from an early Gaelic original. His scepticism, based on Macpherson's failure to produce the originals for inspection, drew a protest from Macpherson to which Johnson sent a reply that was at once forceful and comprehensive:

Mr. James Macpherson – I received your foolish and impudent note. Whatever insult is offered me I will do my best to repel, and what I cannot do for myself the law will do for me. I will not desist from detecting what I think a cheat from any fear of the menaces of a Ruffian.

You want me to retract. What shall I retract? I thought your book an imposture from the beginning. I think it upon yet surer reasons an imposture still. For this opinion I give the publick my reasons which I here dare you to refute.

But however I may despise you, I reverence truth and if you can prove the genuineness of the work I will confess it. Your rage I defy, your abilities since your Homer are not so formidable, and what I have heard of your morals disposes me to pay regard not to what you shall say, but to what you can prove.

You may print this if you will.

Sam: Johnson.

Jan 20, 1775

Perhaps the most famous of the fabricators who insisted that their works were discoveries and not original works was Thomas Chatterton. He claimed that his poems were the work of Thomas Rowley, a monk living near Bristol in the fifteenth century, and that he found them in an old chest belonging to the Church of St Mary Redcliffe at Bristol. Critics called attention to their linguistic inconsistencies, and Chatterton, stung by his lack of recognition, committed suicide at the age of eighteen.

Besides the books that were published with the intention to deceive, there were books like *Robinson Crusoe*, *Gulliver's Travels*, Defoe's *Journal of the Plague Year* and Paltock's *The Life and Adventures of Peter Wilkins*, where it was a literary convention to provide the book with a fictitious setting which probably did not deceive its readers for a moment.

The rewards of forgery are not merely financial, and the motives of literary forgers make a fascinating study. One of the attractions of forgery is undoubtedly the exercise of craftsmanship in the manufacture of the forged document or book quite apart from the prospect of financial reward. When the forger finds that people are willing to pay good money for his productions, he has an added incentive. Some such mixture of motives undoubtedly influenced William Henry Ireland (1777–1835), the forger of Shakespearean documents. His father, Samuel, was an engraver and dealer in prints and drawings who said that his greatest ambition was to find an autograph manuscript of Shakespeare. William, a good son, provided him with one. He was articled to a conveyancer and it was part of his daily work to study old documents. He found a piece of unused parchment at the end of an old rent roll and, after practising Elizabethan penmanship, he produced a lease to which Shakespeare was one of the parties. The signature was copied from a printed facsimile. Old seals torn from earlier documents were appended. His father accepted it as genuine and Willlam supplied him with many collectors' items: verses and letters with Shakespeare's signature written on fly-leaves torn from Elizabethan books, and early printed books with Shakespeare's name on the title-pages, a transcript of *King Lear* with a few alterations from the printed text and a few extracts from *Hamlet*. The orthography, imitated from Chatterton's Rowley Poems, showed a reckless doubling of consonants and frequent additions of final -*e*. To explain provenance William invented a rich gentleman who had placed the documents at his disposal on the condition that his name was not to be mentioned beyond the initials 'M.H.'

In February 1795 the elder Ireland arranged all the documents for exhibition at his house and invited well-known scholars to see them. Boswell kissed the supposed relics on his knees. Twenty eminent men, including Henry James Pye, the Poet Laureate, signed a document testifying to their belief in the genuineness of the manuscripts.

William grew more ambitious and presented his father with a new blank-verse play, *Vortigern and Rowena*, in what he claimed to be Shakespeare's autograph and a tragedy, *Henry II*, which he claimed to have copied from an original in Shakespeare's handwriting. He produced a series of deeds to show that an ancestor with the same name as himself had rescued Shakespeare from drowning and had been rewarded by the dramatist with all the manuscripts that William had brought to light.

From the first there were sceptics, including Joseph Ritson, the antiquary, and Edmund Malone, the Shakespearean scholar. Sheridan had agreed to produce *Vortigern* at Drury Lane and Ireland was to receive £250 and a share of the profits. The play was produced on 2 April 1796, young Ireland resisting an attempt to have it produced on April Fool's Day. It was greeted with ridicule, which increased the number of the sceptics. Both the Irelands were suspected of the forgeries. After questioning, William admitted his guilt and published *An Authentic Account of the Shakespearian MSS* to exculpate his father, who still refused to believe that William, a boy of nineteen, could have executed all the forgeries. On 29 October 1796 Samuel was ridiculed on the stage at Covent Garden as Sir Bamber Blackletter in Reynolds's *Fool of Fortune*. He died in July 1800 still declaring his innocence, though most of the public had lost interest.

Alan G. Thomas[1] gives an account of an elaborate hoax which deceived many collectors and booksellers in 1840. A catalogue was published advertising the forthcoming sale by auction of the collection of a Count J. N. A. de Fortsas, who was said to have bought only unique books. The sale was to take place at Binche, a small town in Belgium. Each of the fifty-two lots was designed to appeal to a leading collector who received a copy of the catalogue. Shortly before the date of the sale an announcement was published that it was cancelled because the people of Binche had combined to buy the entire collection for their public library. The whole thing was a hoax, but among the letters which it evoked was one written by the Princess de Ligne to her bookseller after hearing that one of the items consisted of the very frank memoirs of one of her ancestors: 'Achetez, je vous en conjure, à tout prix les sottises de notre polisson de grand père.' The catalogue, of which a hundred copies were printed, is now a collectors' item and it has been forged. The hoax was the work of René Chalons of Brussels.

Vrain Lucas created his forgeries shortly after the middle of

[1] *Great Books and Book Collectors*, pp. 248–50.

the nineteenth century to sell to a noted mathematician, Michel Charles, over a period of eight years. Lucas confessed to having forged more than twenty-five thousand autographs. Charles doubted his word only once and, when Lucas offered to buy back everything he had sold him, Charles's faith was restored. The forgeries are a monument to human gullibility. One of them was from Pascal to Isaac Newton proving that Pascal, not Newton, had discovered the law of gravitation. At the supposed date of the letter Newton was ten years old. Lucas was tried before a tribunal in 1870 and Charles gave evidence that he had paid 140,000 francs for letters from Dante, Cervantes, Shakespeare, Julius Caesar, and many others, all written in Modern French. After that it is an anti-climax to mention that they were written on paper from local mills with the watermarks of Angoulême.

The most important and sensational series of literary forgeries to have been exposed during the present century is that now known as the Wise forgeries, although the book which brought the forgeries to light does not directly accuse Thomas James Wise of the fabrications. Its title reads almost like a parody of that of an academic dissertation. Conscious of the explosive nature of the facts that they were to reveal, its authors, John Carter and Graham Pollard, seemed to take pleasure in avoiding the sensational in their sober title *An Enquiry into the Nature of Certain Nineteenth Century Pamphlets* (Constable, 1934). The Wise forgeries are important because of the eminence of the forger, the wide range of authors whose work was forged and, most of all, the skill which Carter and Pollard showed in examining the evidence. Their book has become a classic of scholarship in its illustration of the application of modern bibliographical techniques.

We now think of Wise as a forger, but his malpractices were exposed only a few years before his death. For most of his life he was known as an eminent bibliographer who, by his flair as a collector, had built up the outstanding Ashley Library. Most collectors are willing to be diverted from their pursuit of a particular book if they find something else that interests them at an attractive price, but Edmund Gosse compared Wise with an angler who caught a salmon by accident and threw it in again because when he was out to fish for perch he wished to catch perch.

Since Wise was at the time of his exposure very much an establishment figure with a worldwide reputation, there was a need for care in presenting the case and there was room for all sorts of subtle ironies in its presentation. For example, in place of a dedication there was a quotation from Thomas J. Wise's *Bibliography of Swinburne:*

> The whole thing proves once more that, easy as it appears to be to fabricate reprints of rare books, it is in actual practice absolutely impossible to do so in such a manner that detection cannot follow the result.

The starting point of the investigation was the suggestion that the privately-printed first edition of Mrs Browning's 'Sonnets from the Portuguese' (*Sonnets by E.B.B.*, Reading, 1847) was not all that it pretended to be. It was one of about forty pamphlets of similar date which turned up from time to time in auction sales and in the catalogues of certain booksellers, always in fine condition. Such supplies of authentic books can turn up if a bookseller or a speculator has hoarded his unsold stock, hoping to release it gradually and so avoid flooding the market, but the frequent appearance of such items is an indication that further investigation might be rewarding.

One of the remarkable things about the exposure of Wise is that more than thirty years before the publication of Carter and Pollard's *Enquiry*, Cook and Wedderburn in their monumental edition of Ruskin had pointed out that two pamphlets by Ruskin, *The Queen's Gardens* (1864) and *The National Gallery* (1852) were fakes that had been set up from later editions. These important discoveries had been reported so unobtrusively in small-type notes that no one paid any

attention to them, and Carter and Pollard point out, with
characteristic irony, that 'even Mr. Thomas J. Wise, the bibliographer of Ruskin, makes no reference to them'. These
pamphlets by Ruskin are included among those which
seemed to have some resemblances to the Reading edition of
Sonnets by E.B.B.

The reasons for suspecting the authenticity of the Reading
Sonnets by E.B.B. include a number of considerations that fall
very far short of proof. Suspicion is aroused by such negative
evidence as the absence of any recorded copy with an
inscription from either the author or her husband, though the
Brownings inscribed their books quite freely and 'it is an
axiom of book collecting that surviving copies of a privately
printed book exhibit a far higher proportion of presentation
copies to the total number recorded, than a book published
in the ordinary way'.[1] Moreover, no copy is recorded with
any contemporary inscription or mark of ownership. All the
copies coming on the market were clean and in good condition and none of them had a pedigree that could be traced
back earlier than 1890. Not a single copy underwent the fate of
most surviving Victorian pamphlets of being bound up with
other pamphlets with edges trimmed. All the bound copies
are in modern bindings. It throws an interesting light on the
history of book-collecting that when Carter and Pollard
wanted to examine a copy of the Reading *Sonnets*, they had
difficulty in finding one because nearly all the known copies
were in America.

To find positive evidence of forgery it was necessary to
examine the paper and the typography and to collate the text
to find whether it was set up from a copy later than the first
edition. The paper used was identified under a microscope.
The new materials used in the second half of the nineteenth
century included esparto (1860-70), ground wood pulp
(1870-80) and the wood celluloses (1880-90). The paper used

---

[1] Carter and Pollard, op. cit., p. 20.

in the suspected pamphlets aroused suspicions. Paper containing esparto must have been made after 1861 and printing paper containing chemical wood after 1874. One of the suspected pamphlets was made of pure rag paper but ten of them, dated before 1861, contained esparto, and thirteen, dated before 1874, contained chemical wood.

Differences in type design can be precisely dated from the specimen books issued by typefounders. These differences can identify the typefounder but not the printer, since the typefounder may have distributed identical founts to several different printers. Most of the pamphlets are set in a 'modern style', which has only two kerned letters in its lower-case roman, *f* and *j*.[1] The printer Richard Clay persuaded the typefounders P. M. Shanks & Co. to cut for him, some time after 1880, the first design for a lower-case *f* without a kern. Sixteen of the pamphlets, all dated before 1874, were printed in a kernless fount.

Another typographical feature of the Reading *Sonnets* was a distinctive question-mark with a narrow upper arm. The *Sonnets* was printed from a mixed fount containing kernless *f* and *j* as well as this distinctive question-mark. By a lucky accident the investigators found that the mixed fount had been used in printing a facsimile of Matthew Arnold's *Alaric at Rome* edited by Thomas J. Wise in 1893. The printers reported that this type was cast by them in 1876.

Further evidence was obtained by collating the suspected pamphlets with texts that had been revised by their authors. Ruskin's *Of Queen's Gardens* was published in 1865 but Ruskin revised it in 1871. The '1864' pamphlet agrees with the 1871 text against that of the first edition of 1865.

The explanation of Wise's success is that he realized that a forger is more likely to escape detection if he invents an edition instead of copying a known edition which is available

---

[1] A kerned letter is one in which a portion of the face of a letter extends beyond its body. The thin projection of the kern is liable to be chipped off.

for comparison with the imitation by any subsequent investigator. All Wise's forgeries followed a single pattern: he took a short piece from a published volume and printed it in pamphlet form with an earlier date and thus created a fictitious first edition for the collectors' market.

Carter denied that fear of the libel laws was the reason why he did not in 1934 accuse Wise of full responsibility. Any reader of detective stories is familiar with the distinction between knowing who did the deed and being able to prove it. In 1934 Carter and Pollard were in the position of the policeman who has identified the criminal but fears that he cannot convince a jury. Circumstantial evidence continued to pile up, and Wise's guilt is now generally accepted. His former office boy turned bookseller, Herbert Gorfin, had acted as his agent in the distribution of the pamphlets and had provided sworn evidence for Carter and Pollard. In an attempt to suppress the evidence, Wise offered Gorfin £25 for his unsold stock of the pamphlets, raising his offer the next day to £400. This offer was accepted, and the pamphlets were burned in the presence of Wise's lawyers.

The material chosen for forging was that likely to appeal to collectors during the period 1885–95; the minor works of major authors. It was prudent to avoid their major works, since long works were expensive to reproduce and works of high literary value were more likely to have a known history. Ruskin and Stevenson were ill and Swinburne was living in seclusion; Morris was alive and well but the forger assumed, rightly, that he would not be interested enough to protest.

Carter and Pollard did not exactly say that Wise was the forger but they did say of the forger:

> But it seems quite certain that he was successful in planting the forgeries on Mr Wise, in bulk, over a period of at least fourteen years. As events proved, he could have chosen no more influential person for his purpose – the bibliographical and com-

mercial promotion of the forgeries; and he was certainly alive to the vital importance to his scheme of some such unwitting accessory after the fact.[1]

Quite apart from the question of forgery, the investigations of Carter and Pollard revealed the dangers of allowing a bibliographer to be an amateur bookseller. In an article published in 1894 Wise described Browning's *Gold Hair* as 'a privately printed pamphlet of the greatest rarity', but fifteen years later his stock of the pamphlet amounted to at least nineteen, while of Matthew Arnold's *Geist's Grave*, which he described as a rarity in 1894, he was able in 1910 to sell forty-three copies to the bookseller Gorfin. The proclamation that the pamphlets were rarities was made under his own name while the marketing of his stock was carried on largely through agents.

Carter and Pollard were outspoken in commenting on Wise's shortcomings:

> Mr Wise, by his credulity, by his vanity in his own possessions, by his dogmatism, by abuse of his eminence in the bibliographical world, has dealt a blow to the prestige of an honourable science, the repercussions of which will be long and widely felt.[2]

A rather pathetic contrast to this opinion is provided by the reply of the bookseller Gorfin, when accused of selling forgeries: 'Oh, but they can't be. I bought them all from Mr. Wise.' Wise died in 1937, three years after the exposure of his forgeries.

[1] op. cit., pp. 123f.
[2] op. cit., p. 141.

CHAPTER IX

THE DISPOSAL OF A COLLECTION

A PROBLEM that confronts book-collectors is what is to happen to their books after their death. If the collection is small there is no particular problem, but if it is large or nearly complete within its field there is always a strong temptation to keep it together by presenting it to a large public library. There is a tendency for all important books and manuscripts to finish up in one of the great national libraries. For a scholar it is obviously convenient to have under one roof all the books that he wants to consult, but there are disadvantages in too much centralization, and the atomic bomb has provided another argument in favour of dispersal. Probably the solution to the problem lies in an extension of the already considerable use of photographic reproduction. Those who live and work in London, Oxford or Cambridge sometimes take their good fortune for granted and seem indifferent to the competing claims of scholars who live elsewhere. It is time to begin protesting against the growth of an academic great wen in London and to encourage the growth of libraries in other parts of the United Kingdom. Collectors disposing of their libraries can do much to improve the lot of the under-privileged regions and of parts of the world like Australia which, by the accident of history, did not have the same opportunities as libraries in London to build up their collections.

The distinction between disposing of a collection by auction and leaving it to an institution is not clear cut. When a collection is sold by auction, institutions are among the bidders. On the other hand, it cannot be assumed that a library left to an institution will stay there for ever. Public libraries have been known to sell books that have been left to them, though they generally try to dispose of them discreetly because they know that such sales will discourage further bequests. The danger in such secret sales is that the books are liable to be sold more cheaply than if they are disposed of openly. Some collectors make a virtue of dispersal, saying that to present one's library to an institution is to deprive future generations of collectors of the pleasure of hunting for the books and possessing them. This argument would have more validity if books were like land, fixed in quantity. But so long as new books are published in their present quantities, there is going to be no shortage of books for posterity to collect. In certain fields it is now impossible for a collector to build up a comprehensive collection. The remedy is easy: choose some other field. A volume of essays by various hands, *New Paths in Book-Collecting* (Constable, 1934), contained many suggestions for new fields, and the number of possibilities is endless. The most obvious new field would be one that did not exist when the great collections of the past were being formed; modern first editions appeal to many collectors, for example.

The weakness of the argument that collections should be broken up for the benefit of future book-buyers is that it involves a good deal of wasted effort. One of the arguments in favour of collecting is that a large collection of related items is more useful to students than the same books would be if dispersed. The break-up of collections may sometimes be necessary, but it is to be hoped that some of them will remain as special collections in larger libraries. Another argument in favour of this practice is that the building up of an important collection may well take more than a single life-time. If the collection is bequeathed or sold as a collection it can form a nucleus for future growth. At a more humble level, booksellers will sometimes offer a collection of books by or about a single author without pricing the items separately.

The strongest reason for not bequeathing one's library to an institution is that it is more than likely that the institution doesn't want it, especially if the gift is hedged round with the stipulations that collectors like to make to ensure the separate identity of their collections after their death. Such stipulations as the requirement that the books shall be kept together or that duplicates shall not be sold are sometimes made, but one can understand the point of view of a librarian who thinks that a miscellaneous collection of fairly common books is not worth accepting if such conditions are attached. The collector who wishes to present his collection to a public library ought to make his plans early by forming a collection that a public library may be expected to covet.

Donors do not always realize that the gift of a whole private library may be an embarrassment to a librarian, because the cost of cataloguing and housing a book may be more than the value of the book itself. At some libraries gifts are selected as rigorously as purchases in order to avoid unnecessary storage costs. The mere fact that the library already has a copy of a book is no reason for refusing it, since a library often needs duplicates, but the duplicates should be selected according to the needs of the library not according to the accident of donation. The most useful way in which a testator can bequeath his books to a library is to give the library the chance to select the books that it needs, and the offer might well be made to a number of libraries in turn. Before a gift of books is accepted, it should be made clear whether the library has the right to dispose of duplicates, and only collections of outstanding importance should be accepted without this right.

If a collection is to be made attractive to the library to which it is offered, the first requirement is a worthwhile subject and the second is reasonable completeness within the chosen field. For this purpose it is necessary for most of us to choose a subject of limited scope, such as books by or about one particular author, preferably not Shakespeare. If a collection really is a special collection, in the sense that it is not only more complete than others sections of the same library but that it can stand comparison with other collections on the same subject anywhere in the world, it is fairly certain that many public and university libraries, in Great Britain and America, will be glad to have it and that the library that acquires it will be willing to treat it as a special collection.

The highly specialized collection, as distinct from a scholar's working library, deserves special treatment by libraries. Everything possible should be done to encourage collectors to bequeath such collections, and the promise not to dispose of duplicates or the provision of a special book-plate are small prices to pay to attract collections which may provide the basis for important research.

Just as the National Trust has to be cautious about accepting properties unless provision is made for their upkeep, so the gift of a collection to a library might very well be accompanied by the gift of a sum of money to pay for the cost of cataloguing the collection and keeping it up-to-date. In making this suggestion I am confident that I can count on the warm support of librarians. I am less confident of their support when I suggest that the sum necessary for the endowment of the collection might well be extracted from the library itself by selling the collection to the library, possibly at a price lower than the market price, and by settling the sum thus extracted upon the library with the stipulation that it shall be earmarked for the cataloguing and bringing up-to-date of the collection. Libraries, like human beings, value things that they have had to pay for.

When leaving money to a library for the purchase of books, there is something to be said for stipulating that the money or the interest on it must be spent within a specified time. To buy books calls for the expenditure of time and effort on the part of the librarian and it is sometimes well to deprive him of the temptation to hoard his reserve funds.

American libraries are more ready than British to put on special exhibitions and to woo the collector to leave his collection to an institution. Libraries can advise collectors and may themselves be advised by holders of university chairs. Chauncey Brewster Tinker combined a Chair of English

Literature with the office of Keeper of Rare Books in Yale University Library, and Wilmarth Lewis's Horace Walpole collection has close links with the same library.

Donors are more ready to present outstanding single items to a library than run of the mill books or learned periodicals, but libraries have their own funds to pay for routine purchases. University libraries are beginning to pay more attention to their rare book rooms and this increased interest is sending up prices.

Only a small proportion of collections are important enough to be treated in this way; for most private libraries dispersal is the inevitable end. The two practicable methods are auction and sale to a bookseller. If the collection has little value the former method is ruled out, since an auctioneer of standing is not likely to want to sell bulky lots when his commission does not cover the cost of handling. When a collection is valuable enough to be sold by auction, the record of prices realized gives an indication of the state of the market, which is a useful guide to other potential sellers, but it is a guide that has to be used with caution. A record of prices is useless unless it is dated, and to have much value it must be recent. The prices in William Lowndes's *The Bibliographer's Manual* (1834) are of interest only to the economic historian or the student of the history of collecting. The prices in *Book Auction Records* have more relevance for the book-buyer of today, but the record may fail to mention that a book has fetched a high price because it has a valuable autograph on the title-page or a low one because it is in poor condition. In the excitement of a sale two bidders may lose their heads and bid a book far above its value. The successful bidder at such a sale offered his acquisition to the underbidder at the price that he had bid, to receive the frosty reply: 'Since the sale I have come to my senses.' For all these reasons it is best not to pay too much attention to a single auction price, but if a book consistently realizes a high price, that price may be accepted as its current value.

Booksellers sometimes complain of the customer, often an

executor, who begins by saying that he has no idea of the value of the books that he wants to sell, but when he receives an offer shows that he has quite a precise idea of what they are worth. After an offer is made he discloses that he is under an obligation to consult somebody else. Percy Muir, a fair-minded man, comments: 'It is, perhaps, not to be greatly wondered at that some booksellers regard such vendors as their legitimate prey.'[1] But it is not clear why these two actions of the customer should be regarded as an adequate excuse for retaliation. The real offence is the attempt to get a free valuation, and the bookseller's safeguard is to say that if he makes an offer he will charge an agreed fee unless the books are ultimately sold to him. Most customers who offend in this way do so from a failure to see the transaction from the book-seller's point of view and have no idea that they are behaving badly, but the executor's problem is not adequately solved if he simply accepts the offer of the first bookseller consulted. I have been offered £30, £100 and nothing at all for the same set of books on the same day. If the collection of books is not valuable enough to be catalogued for sale by auction, the vendor's best course of action is to pay for a valuation, pro-vided that he can induce a bookseller to undertake the task.

A bookseller who makes an offer that is not accepted is entitled to a fee, unless his offer is so low that he is shown to be either a rogue or an incompetent valuer. One solution of the problem is to pay one bookseller for a valuation in the know-ledge that the books will then be sold to another. The difficulty here is that booksellers are not too anxious to value books even for a fee. At a time when books are scarce most book-sellers would rather be the man to whom the collection is offered than the one who is paid for a valuation. Wide varia-tions in the prices offered for books are only to be expected. The price that a bookseller offers for a book is its value *to him*, and he may feel that he cannot afford the shelf-room to keep

[1] Percy H. Muir, *Minding My Own Business* (Chatto & Windus, 1956), p. 209.

a set of books in stock for a long time unless his margin of profit is very high indeed.

To have a good understanding with a bookseller is very useful when a collector wants to sell his books. Fortunately most of us have done our book-buying in a rising market, and consequently we have had the pleasant experience of selling books for more than we gave for them.

There is no need for a collector to wait until he is at the point of death before beginning the dispersal of a library. Many people declare proudly that they never sell a book. Some of them could add, with equal truth, that they don't often buy one either, but to keep unwanted books is nothing to be proud of. The collector's interests change and, as he gets older, the feeling of immortality which attended him in his youth begins to wear off and he realizes that he is not going to live long enough to read all the books that he once hoped to read. Ruskin had no hesitation in disposing of books when he had finished with them, and he relieved his feelings by adding frank inscriptions giving his reasons for selling. Examples are: 'Old school book not *opened* these thirty years', 'Thrown out through want of room, never a word read', and 'Thrown out with other rubbish'.[1] Maurice Baring's solution to the problem was more drastic. Whenever he moved into a new house, he threw away all his books and started a new library. Those who feel inclined to follow his example should reflect that to throw away a library of any size is no easy task. Max Beerbohm has described the difficulty that he had in burning even a single book, and the patience of dustmen is not inexhaustible. The difficulty is that most people find it hard to forecast the future direction of their interests, and human perversity is such that the sale of a book is enough to revive what one had assumed to be a forgotten interest. There are other reasons for selling books, the most common of which is shortage of shelf-room. Other reasons are that a collector may have bought lots at auction that include books that he does

[1] *The Book Collector*, 1972, p. 212.

not want or his wife may have finally put her foot down. One man who had been proudly displaying his library to a fellow collector was disconcerted when his friend pointed to three empty shelves and said: 'You know, I envy you those three empty shelves more than all the books in your library.'

At one time I had about twenty thousand books, which was too many. By hard work and with the co-operation of librarians and booksellers I have reduced the number to twelve thousand, which is still too many. The normal fate of a miscellaneous collection of books is sale to a bookseller or possibly to more than one bookseller. A member of a large firm of booksellers once described a visit that he had paid to the widow of an eminent scholar. He reported with surprise that the library consisted of the sort of books that can be found on any bookstall and were hardly worth the trouble of carting away. He seems not to have considered the likelihood that he had been invited to inspect the remnant of a library after other booksellers had picked out all the saleable books. One can sympathize with the bookseller, who felt that his time had been wasted, but if the executors did dispose of the library in this way, they probably got a better price for it than they would have done if they had offered the whole collection to a dealer in cheap books. Booksellers tend to specialize, and to a non-academic bookseller piles of paper-backed German dissertations would probably seem so much waste paper, whereas a specialist bookseller might be able to give, and ask, a high price for such material.

One of the bookseller's chief problems is the shop-lifter. Another is the customer who treats a bookshop as a reference library and shows no recognition of a responsibility to buy the books that he enjoys dipping into. The two categories merge into one when a browser absent-mindedly walks off with the book that he has been reading. Second-hand booksellers often leave a shelf of books outside the shop to tempt passers-by to browse, and books thus exposed are especially vulnerable. One disgusted north-country bookseller who found that a book had been stolen five minutes after he had put it on display was heard to mutter: 'Nay, they don't give you time to put 'em out now.'

It is some satisfaction to a book-collector to think that after his death his books will be of use to others. He may then hope to look down from whatever heaven book-collectors go to when they die (looking something like Blackwell's), and reflect that, in the words of Hilaire Belloc, his sins were scarlet but his books were read.

SELECT BIBLIOGRAPHY

Books especially recommended are marked with an asterisk.

The Book Collector, incorporating *Book Handbook*, ed. Ian Fleming, John Hayward and P. H. Muir, Queen Anne Press 1952 – a quarterly, still in progress.

CARTER, JOHN (ed.), *New Paths in Book Collecting: Essays by Various Hands*, Constable 1934.

*CARTER, JOHN, *Taste and Technique in Book-Collecting*, CUP 1948.

CARTER, JOHN, *Books and Book-Collectors*, Rupert Hart-Davis, 1956.

CARTER, JOHN, *ABC for Book Collectors*, 5th edn, Rupert Hart-Davis 1972.

CARTER, JOHN, and POLLARD, GRAHAM, *An Enquiry into the Nature of Certain Nineteenth Century Pamphlets*, Constable 1934.

COLLISON, ROBERT L., *Book Collecting: An Introduction to Modern Methods of Literary and Bibliographical Detection*, Ernest Benn 1957.

DARTON, F. J. HARVEY, *Children's Books in England: Five Centuries of Social Life*, 2nd edn, CUP 1958.

GASKELL, PHILIP, *A New Introduction to Bibliography*, OUP 1972.

HORROX, REGINALD (ed.), *Book Handbook: An Illustrated Guide to Old and Rare Books*, Horrox, Bracknell, Berks 1951.
This volume was issued serially in nine parts from 1947 to 1949.

JACKSON, HOLBROOK, *The Anatomy of Bibliomania*, 3rd edn, Soncino Press 1932.

LEWIS, WILMARTH, *Collector's Progress*, Constable 1952.

McKERROW, RONALD B., *An Introduction to Bibliography for Literature Students*, OUP 1927.

*MUIR, PERCY H., *Book-Collecting as a Hobby in a Series of Letters to Everyman*, Gramol Publications 1944.

MUIR, PERCY H., *Book-Collecting: More Letters to Everyman*, Cassell 1949.

MUIR, PERCY H. (ed.), *Talks on Book-Collecting*, Cassell 1952.

MUNBY, A. N. L., *Phillipps Studies*, 5 vols, CUP 1951–60.

NEWTON, A. EDWARD, *A Magnificent Farce and Other Diversions of a Book-Collector*, Putnam 1921.

NEWTON, A. EDWARD, *This Book-Collecting Game*, Routledge 1930.

ROSENBACH, A. S. W., *Books and Bidders: The Adventures of a Bibliophile*, George Allen & Unwin 1928.

The Rothschild Library: A Catalogue of the Collection of Eighteenth-Century Printed Books and Manuscripts formed by Lord Rothschild, 2 vols., CUP 1954.

SADLEIR, MICHAEL, *Book Collecting: A Reader's Guide*, OUP for National Book League 1947.

SADLEIR, MICHAEL, *XIX Century Fiction: A Bibliographical Guide*, 2 vols, CUP 1951.

*THOMAS, ALAN G., *Great Books and Book Collectors*, Weidenfeld & Nicolson 1975.

WINTERICH, JOHN T., *A Primer of Book-Collecting*, edited for English collectors by Raymond Dean, George Allen & Unwin 1928.

WOLF, EDWIN and FLEMING, JOHN F., *Rosenbach: A Biography*, Weidenfeld & Nicolson 1960.

GLOSSARY

ART PAPER. Paper with a glossy or coated surface, suitable for the reproduction of illustrations.

ASSOCIATION COPY. Copy of a book which once belonged to the author or which has been in the possession of one of his friends or of someone with a special interest in its contents.

BLIND TOOLING. Ornamentation of a book-cover with designs impressed by heated tools without the use of a press and without the addition of gilding or colour.

BLOCKING. Ornamentation of a book-cover by the application of a piece of metal bearing an engraved design and intended for use in a press, as distinct from tooling, in which the metal implements are applied by hand.

BLURB. Publisher's brief description of a book printed on its jacket.

BROADSIDE or BROADSHEET. A large sheet of paper printed on only one side.

CALENDERING. Pressing paper by rollers in a machine to glaze or smooth it.

CANCEL. A leaf, part of a leaf or group of leaves substituted for what was originally printed.

CASING. A substitute for binding which is used in the production of the vast majority of modern books. The case is made separately, and the stitched gatherings, held together by a strip of canvas, are inserted into the ready-made case by machinery.

CASLON. A style of type cut by the Caslons, father and son, eighteenth-century typographers, or one imitated from their type.

CHAIN LINES. Widely-spaced lines, visible in the texture of LAID PAPER, made by the wire mesh at the bottom of the tray in which it is made.

CHAINED LIBRARIES. Medieval libraries in which books were chained to their shelves as a precaution against theft.

CHASE. The metal frame holding composed type and locking it in position.

COLLATION. Detailed comparison verifying the order of sheets by examination of the SIGNATURES. The word is also used to denote the bibliographical description of the physical composition of a book.

COLOPHON. A note at the end of an early printed book giving the title of the work and its author, printer and place of printing.

EDITION. All the copies of a book produced, except for very minor corrections, from one setting of the type at any time.

END-PAPERS. Double leaves added by a binder at the front and back of a book, the outer leaf being pasted to the inner surface of the cover and the inner leaf forming the first or last leaf of the bound volume.

FLY-LEAF. A blank leaf at the beginning or end of a book.

FLY-TITLE. A second HALF-TITLE sometimes found between the last page of the PRELIMS and the opening page of the text. The term is sometimes used to denote a separate title-page which may introduce a section or division of a book.

FOLIO. Book made up of sheets folded only once.

FORE-EDGE. The vertical edge of a page furthest away from the spine. In some old books the fore-edges are decorated with a painting applied when the leaves are slightly fanned out and then held fast. The edges are then squared up and gilded over, so that the painting is visible only when the book is open and the pages spread.

FOXING. Brown spot or stain on paper, caused by damp or lack of ventilation.

FRIABLE. Easily crumbled (of paper).

GATHERING. Group of leaves brought together after the printed sheet has been folded to the size of the book. The gathering forms a unit in book-binding.

GHOST-TITLE. Title of a book that has been advertised but never published.

GOTHIC. Old-fashioned type found in early printed books and many German books, characterized by thick down-strokes. It is sometimes called Black Letter. Today it is used chiefly in the titles of some newspapers.

HALF BINDING. Binding in which leather is used for the spine and outer corners while the sides are covered with cloth or paper. See QUARTER BINDING.

HALF-TITLE. The leaf in front of the title-page, which records the title, usually without further details.

HALF-TONE. Illustration printed from a block, produced by photographic means, in which the light and shade of the original are represented by dots of varying sizes.

IMPRESSION. All the copies of a book produced from one setting of the type at one time.

ITALIC. Thin, sloping type introduced by Aldus Manutius of Venice c. 1500, used today for emphasis or to indicate foreign words.

KERN. Part of metal type projecting beyond the body of the letter.

LAID PAPER. Paper made on a mesh of close-set parallel wires, which leave marks that are visible when the paper is held up to the light.

LOWER CASE. Small letters, as distinct from capitals.

MILLBOARD. Stout PASTEBOARD, used for bookbinding.

OCTAVO. Book made up of sheets folded three times, to form leaves each of which is one-eighth of the size of the original sheet.

OLD FACE. An early form of hand-designed type following calligraphic models, with thickening and thinning in imitation of the action of the pen. The capitals are below the height of the ascending letters.

PASTEBOARD. Stiff substance for bookbinding, made by pasting sheets of paper together.

PASTE-DOWN. That half of an ENDPAPER which is pasted to the cover of a book.

PICA. Unit of type-size, one-sixth of an inch in height, now generally called '12-point'.

POINT. (1) Distinctive feature of type or the physical characteristics of a book that makes it possible to distinguish one variant from another.

(2) As an indication of the size of type, one seventy-second of an inch. Usually preceded by a figure; for example, 12-point type is one-sixth of an inch tall.

PRELIMS. The leaves which precede the actual text, including the title-page, list of contents, dedication and preface. They are usually the last part of a book to be printed.

PUBLISHER'S CLOTH. Cloth used by publishers for binding or casing books before sale. It became general in British and American publishing between 1825 and 1835. Previously books had generally been issued in paper-covered boards as a temporary measure until they could be bound in leather to the order of the purchaser.

QUARTER BINDING. Binding in which leather is used for the spine but not for the corners. See HALF BINDING.

QUARTO. Book made up of sheets folded twice to form leaves each of which is one-quarter of the size of the original sheet.

QUIRE. Collection of leaves folded one within another in a book, sometimes called a GATHERING.

RECTO. The right-hand page of an open book or manuscript.

REMAINDERS. Copies of a book left unsold when demand has almost ceased and offered for sale at a reduced price.

ROMAN TYPE. Plain upright type normally used in printed books today, as distinct from GOTHIC and ITALIC.

RUNNING TITLE. A line of type at the top of a page, above the text, consisting of the title of a book or a section of a book.

SIGNATURE. Letter or figure placed at the foot of a page, usually the first leaf of each gathering, as a guide to the binder.

SOLANDER CASE. A book-shaped box with a tightly-fitting upper portion fitting over the neck of the lower portion. It was invented by Daniel Charles Solander (1736–82), a pupil of Linnaeus, for the preservation of botanical specimens.

SOPHISTICATION. Interference with the make-up of a book or manuscript to conceal defects or to improve its appearance.

SPRING-BACK FOLDER. A folder containing a strong spring which holds papers firmly together without the necessity of piercing them.

STATE. Subdivision of an edition showing differences from other copies such that one state cannot be shown to be earlier than other copies of the edition.

SUB-TITLE. Supplementary or additional title of a book.

THREE-DECKER. A book in three volumes, usually a nineteenth-century novel.

UNCUT. With leaves untrimmed by the use of a guillotine.

UNOPENED. With leaves unsevered by the use of a paper-knife

from neighbouring leaves to which they are attached at the top and fore-edges after the folding of a sheet.

VELLUM. The skin of a calf, specially treated to receive writing or printing or as a material for bindings.

VERSO. The left-hand page of an open book or manuscript.

WATERMARK. Faint design visible on some paper when held up to the light. It is produced from a design incorporated in the wire mesh of the tray in which the pulp settles during the process of papermaking.

WIRE LINES. Closely set lines in LAID PAPER, made by the wire mesh of the tray in which the pulp settles during the process of paper-making. They are at right angles to the widely-spaced CHAIN LINES.

WORMING. Holes left in paper, and sometimes in bindings, by the passage of bookworms.

WOVE PAPER. Paper made on a close-meshed wire belt and therefore having a uniform unlined surface, as compared with LAID PAPER.

YAPP. Style of bookbinding with limp leather cover projecting to fold over all three edges of the leaves.

INDEX